Common Core Writing Handbook

Teacher's Guide

GRADE
3

D1540572

Photo Credits

Placement Key: (r) right, (l) left, (c) center, (t) top, (b) bottom, (bg) background

Front cover (cl) PhotoAlto/Getty Images; (tr) Photodisc/Getty Images; (bl) Photodisc/Getty Images; (cr) Comstock/Getty Images; (bc) Image Source/Getty Images.

Back cover (tl) Photodisc/Getty Images; (cl) Photodisc/Getty Images; (cr) Comstock/Getty Images; (br) Adobe Image Library/Getty Images.

Printed in the U.S.A.

ISBN: 978-0-547-86496-9

5 6 7 8 9 10 0982 21 20 19 18 17 16 15 14 13

4500411876   B C D E F G

HOUGHTON MIFFLIN HARCOURT

Contents

Writing Strategies

Writing Models and Forms (continued)

How to Use This Book

The *Common Core Writing Handbook* was designed to complement the writing instruction in your reading program as well as meet all of the Common Core State Standards for writing. It consists of two components: a handbook for students that they can refer to as a resource as well as practice writing in throughout the year, and a Teacher's Guide that supports instruction by providing minilessons for every handbook topic.

Components

Two easy-to-use components make up the *Common Core Writing Handbook* program:

- For Grades 2–6, a 160-page partially consumable student handbook with 30 writing topics that correlate to your reading program's lessons.

The first section of each grade-level handbook includes writing models along with interactive practice to scaffold or reinforce students' understanding of opinion, informational/explanatory, and narrative writing. As students practice writing, they build additional examples of forms to refer to throughout the year as well as develop a deeper understanding of each form's structure.

The second section of the handbook is a resource tool that students can refer to whenever they write. Topics range from writing strategies to how to use technology to do research.

- For Grade 1, a 96-page partially consumable student handbook also includes 30 correlated handbook topics followed by a resource section on writing strategies, such as the writing process and writing traits.

- For Grades K–6, a Teacher's Guide

with 60 minilessons for section 1 (two minilessons for each section 1 student handbook topic) plus one minilesson, as needed, for each remaining page of the resource handbook. The Kindergarten Teacher's Guide includes an abundance of copying masters.

Minilessons

Minilessons are short, focused lessons on specific topics. For each minilesson, you will demonstrate an aspect of writing before students try it. In this Teacher's Guide, minilessons are provided for each topic in the Student Handbook. In the first section are two minilessons for each handbook topic. Each of these minilessons consists of the following parts:

- Topic title
- Tab with section name
- Minilesson number and title
- Common Core State Standards addressed
- Objective and guiding question
- Easy-to-follow instruction in an *I Do*, *We Do*, and *You Do* format
- Modeled, collaborative, and independent writing
- Conference and evaluation information

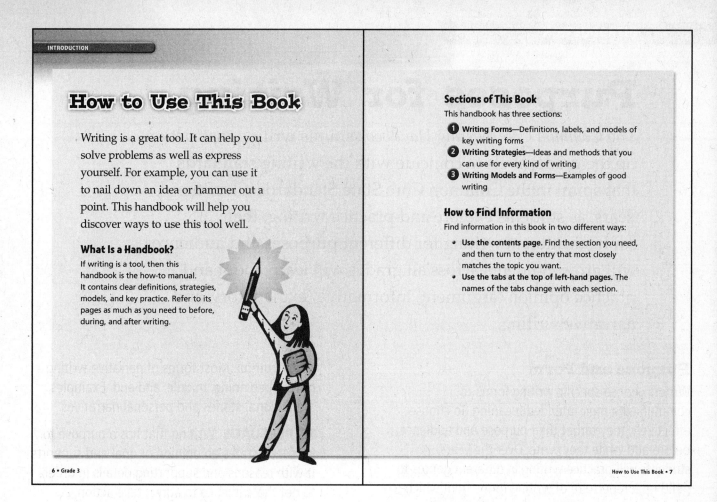

How to Use This Book

Writing is a great tool. It can help you solve problems as well as express yourself. For example, you can use it to nail down an idea or hammer out a point. This handbook will help you discover ways to use this tool well.

What Is a Handbook?

If writing is a tool, then this handbook is the how-to manual. It contains clear definitions, strategies, models, and key practice. Refer to its pages as much as you need to before, during, and after writing.

Sections of This Book

This handbook has three sections:

1. **Writing Forms**—Definitions, labels, and models of key writing forms
2. **Writing Strategies**—Ideas and methods that you can use for every kind of writing
3. **Writing Models and Forms**—Examples of good writing

How to Find Information

Find information in this book in two different ways:

- **Use the contents page.** Find the section you need, and then turn to the entry that most closely matches the topic you want.
- **Use the tabs at the top of left-hand pages.** The names of the tabs change with each section.

- Technology references
- Reduced facsimiles of student handbook pages
- Tips for corrective feedback
- A feature that further explores the lesson's writing trait

Each writing minilesson has been correlated to your reading program's writing lessons so that all mini-lessons and corresponding writing handbook pages within this section are used at least once during the school year. Additional minilessons are provided throughout the Teacher's Guide and correlate to each remaining page in the handbook. Use these minilessons, as needed, to clarify concepts for students and provide additional support.

Student-Page Walk-Through

Have students turn to and read pages 6 and 7 in their books. Explain to them that their handbook is a tool that they can use whenever they write. It can help them find information quickly about any writing question they have, and they can use it to help them during writing. Guide students to find

each of these parts in their handbooks:

- Table of contents
- Introductory pages, including over-views of the writing process and the writing traits
- Writing form pages, each with a section tab, title, definition, and helpful bulleted points, followed by a clear example of the writing model as well as a write-in activity page
- Additional reference pages on topics ranging from writing strategies to revising to using technology, as well as more examples of writing models they may need or want to refer to during the year for projects and other assignments
- An index. Remind students that the table of contents is in order of pre-sentation while the index is ordered alphabetically.

Purposes for Writing

The *Common Core Writing Handbook* spirals writing instruction up the grade levels to coincide with the writing standards that spiral in the Common Core State Standards. Over the years, as students explore and practice writing, their sophistication in writing for different purposes and audiences will grow. Students across all grades will learn about and practice opinion/argument, informative/explanatory, and narrative writing.

Purpose and Form

Writers choose specific writing forms to communicate their intended meaning. To choose effectively, they target their purpose and audience before and while they write. Over the years, students will practice writing in different genres to build up a repertoire of writing forms from which to choose. This increasing practice as well as access to information about writing will help students feel more comfortable about writing and, hopefully, enjoy doing it.

In this handbook, the writing forms and models presented coincide primarily with the purposes expressed through the Common Core State Standards. These are to inform, to explain, to narrate, and to persuade. There are other purposes for writing as well, but these four are emphasized to best prepare students for college and career readiness.

TO INFORM The purpose for writing to inform is to share facts and other information. Informational texts such as reports make statements that are supported by facts and truthful evidence.

TO EXPLAIN The purpose for writing to explain is to tell *what, how,* and *why* about a topic. An example is to explain in writing how to do or make something.

TO NARRATE The purpose of writing to narrate is to tell a story. The story can be made

up or truthful. Most forms of narrative writing have a beginning, middle, and end. Examples are fictional stories and personal narratives.

TO PERSUADE Writing that has a purpose to persuade states an opinion or goal and supports it with reasons and supporting details in order to get the audience to agree, take action, or both. At Grade 6, the emphasis shifts to argument.

Over the years, as their writing grows more sophisticated, students may find that their purpose for writing is a hybrid of two or more purposes. An example would be literary nonfiction that includes elements of storytelling although it may be written primarily to inform and explain. Another example would be historical fiction that tells a story but relates events accurately in order to inform the reader as well.

Success in School and Life

Students and adults are often judged by how well they can communicate. Students are encouraged to learn to write effectively to be successful in their studies. In particular, by the upper grades, they need to master the basic essay format that includes

- An introductory paragraph that identifies the topic or statement of purpose.

- Supporting paragraphs that provide related details and examples.

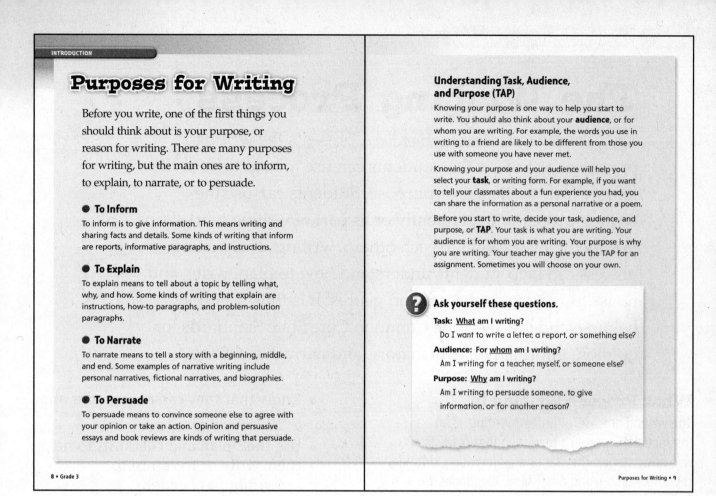

Purposes for Writing

Before you write, one of the first things you should think about is your purpose, or reason for writing. There are many purposes for writing, but the main ones are to inform, to explain, to narrate, or to persuade.

● **To Inform**

To inform is to give information. This means writing and sharing facts and details. Some kinds of writing that inform are reports, informative paragraphs, and instructions.

● **To Explain**

To explain means to tell about a topic by telling what, why, and how. Some kinds of writing that explain are instructions, how-to paragraphs, and problem-solution paragraphs.

● **To Narrate**

To narrate means to tell a story with a beginning, middle, and end. Some examples of narrative writing include personal narratives, fictional narratives, and biographies.

● **To Persuade**

To persuade means to convince someone else to agree with your opinion or take an action. Opinion and persuasive essays and book reviews are kinds of writing that persuade.

Understanding Task, Audience, and Purpose (TAP)

Knowing your purpose is one way to help you start to write. You should also think about your **audience**, or for whom you are writing. For example, the words you use in writing to a friend are likely to be different from those you use with someone you have never met.

Knowing your purpose and your audience will help you select your **task**, or writing form. For example, if you want to tell your classmates about a fun experience you had, you can share the information as a personal narrative or a poem.

Before you start to write, decide your task, audience, and purpose, or **TAP**. Your task is what you are writing. Your audience is for whom you are writing. Your purpose is why you are writing. Your teacher may give you the TAP for an assignment. Sometimes you will choose on your own.

? Ask yourself these questions.

Task: <u>What</u> am I writing?

Do I want to write a letter, a report, or something else?

Audience: For <u>whom</u> am I writing?

Am I writing for a teacher, myself, or someone else?

Purpose: <u>Why</u> am I writing?

Am I writing to persuade someone, to give information, or for another reason?

● A closing paragraph that sums up and concludes.

Students will use this essay form to produce reports, literary analyses, theses, and critiques throughout their academic career. They will also be tested on their ability to write effective essays in standardized tests. In later life, as adults, they will need to be able to communicate clearly in writing to coworkers, bosses, and clients. This requires extensive and ongoing exposure to exemplary writing models and explicit instruction in a variety of areas, as well as opportunities to practice different forms of writing. In all cases, their purpose for writing must be clear. Evidence suggests that the more time student writers spend on writing, developing their writing skills, and deepening their writing experience, the better writers they become.

The Reading-Writing Connection

The ability to communicate their thinking about texts for a variety of purposes and audiences will serve students well in preparation for college and career readiness. When students write about what they read, reflecting on content, craft, or another aspect of a text, they provide evidence of their thinking. This helps teachers know how well students have understood a text. Additionally, the more students write in response to texts, the more they increase their ability to reflect and improve their critical writing ability. Also, students learn to cite evidence from texts in supporting their claims or supporting their main ideas. This ability becomes particularly useful in writing reports and opinion pieces.

Introduce the Purposes

Have students turn to page 8 and read the text. Explain that these are the key purposes for writing that will be explored in their handbooks. Give or elicit an example of a writing form that might be used for each purpose. Examples might include an informational paragraph or a research report *to inform*, directions or a how-to essay *to explain*, a story or personal narrative *to narrate*, and an opinion essay or letter to the editor *to persuade*. Then have students read the next page. Discuss how students should always consider their TAP—or task, audience, and purpose—to help them better target the message of their writing.

The Writing Process

The *Common Core Writing Handbook* presents the writing process as a strategy that students can use to help them write for any task, audience, or purpose. Students can use the writing process independently or as part of writing workshops in which they respond to each other's writing. The writing process can help students understand how to plan, write, and revise for various purposes and genres. It is thus useful in helping students meet the Common Core State Standards for opinion, informative/explanatory, and narrative writing.

What Process Writing Is

The writing process, or process writing, is an instructional approach to writing that consists of five basic stages. The stages are prewriting, drafting, revising, editing, and publishing. The stages are recursive in nature, meaning that students are encouraged to go back and forth between the stages as needed.

The characteristics of the stages of the writing process are as follows:

Prewriting

This is the stage where students begin to plan their writing. Students:

- Define a task and purpose.
- Identify an audience.
- Brainstorm ideas.
- Narrow and choose a topic.
- Plan and organize information.

Drafting

During drafting, students make their first attempt at fleshing out the prewriting idea and forming it into a written work. In other words, students put their ideas in writing. In this stage, students:

- Write a first draft.
- Do not yet worry about perfecting their writing.

- Know that they can revise, edit, and proofread later.
- Use their plan and checklists to help them write or to return to prewriting, as needed.

Revising

A draft is reread and decisions are made to rework and improve it. In this stage, students might:

- Read aloud their work to others to determine how it sounds and how it might be improved.
- Conference with other students.
- Add information.
- Delete unnecessary information.
- Rearrange sentences and paragraphs.
- Combine sentences.

Editing

During editing, the draft is polished. In this stage, students reread and correct their writing for the following:

- Grammar
- Spelling
- Mechanics
- Usage

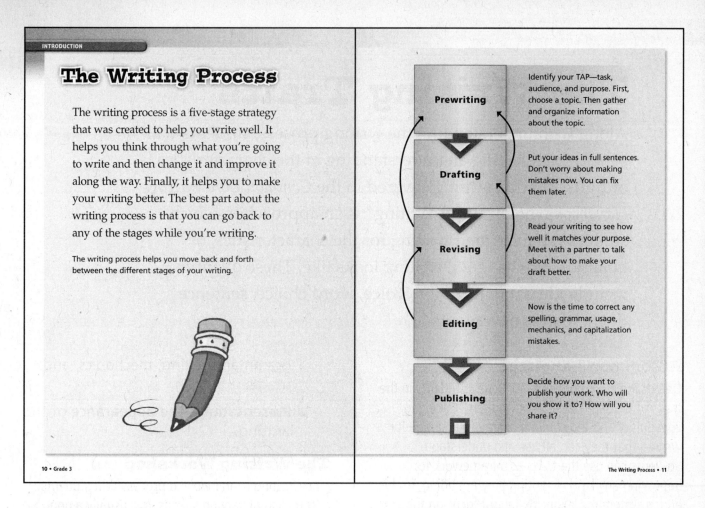

The Writing Process

The writing process is a five-stage strategy that was created to help you write well. It helps you think through what you're going to write and then change it and improve it along the way. Finally, it helps you to make your writing better. The best part about the writing process is that you can go back to any of the stages while you're writing.

The writing process helps you move back and forth between the different stages of your writing.

Prewriting
Identify your TAP—task, audience, and purpose. First, choose a topic. Then gather and organize information about the topic.

Drafting
Put your ideas in full sentences. Don't worry about making mistakes now. You can fix them later.

Revising
Read your writing to see how well it matches your purpose. Meet with a partner to talk about how to make your draft better.

Editing
Now is the time to correct any spelling, grammar, usage, mechanics, and capitalization mistakes.

Publishing
Decide how you want to publish your work. Who will you show it to? How will you share it?

Publishing

Students share their writing with others. In this stage, students typically:

- Make a final, clean copy.
- Use their best handwriting, if writing by hand. If they are sharing their work electronically, they typically choose typefaces and other elements to make their writing readable and attractive.
- Combine their writing with art or graphics.
- Make multiple copies, read their writing aloud, post it electronically, or share and display it in some other way.

Introduce the Process

Have students read pages 10–11. Explain that the writing process is a strategy that they can use to help them write about any topic. Point out how the graphic on page 11 has arrows, indicating that students can go back and forth between the stages

as needed. For students who have no previous orientation to the writing process, simplify your introduction by emphasizing at first only the three key stages of planning, drafting, and revising. Elicit how most tasks of any nature require planning, doing or making something, and then thinking about what might be done better and making those improvements. Compare how these same basic stages can be used each time students write.

Have students turn to the table of contents and locate the section in their handbooks devoted to the writing process (pages 74–81). Explain that they can use these handbook pages whenever they need help with specific stages or writing in general. Point out that each stage in the handbook has one or two pages devoted to it that tell more about the stage. As an example, have students turn to the Prewriting pages 74-75, and point out how they show the different organizational plans students can use for the different kinds of writing they will do. Encourage students to use their handbooks as a resource whenever they write.

The Writing Traits

Along with understanding the writing process, students will benefit from having an understanding of the characteristics, or traits, of good writing covered in the *Common Core Writing Handbook.* The "Traits of Writing" is an approach in which students analyze their writing for the characteristics, or qualities, of what good writing looks like. These qualities include ideas, organization, voice, word choice, sentence fluency, and conventions.

A Common Language

One of the advantages of instructing students in the traits of writing is that you give them a working vocabulary and thus build a common language for writing that they can all use and understand. Students can use the traits as a framework for improving any kind of writing they are doing. To this end, a systematic, explicitly taught focus on the traits of writing has proved to be an effective tool for discussing writing, enabling students to analyze and improve their own writing, and providing teachers with a way to assess students' compositions in a fair, even-handed manner.

Writers typically focus on six traits, with presentation—or the appearance of writing— sometimes considered an additional trait.

- **Ideas**—the meaning and development of the message.

- **Organization**—the structure of the writing.

- **Voice**—the tone of the writing, which reveals the writer's personality and affects the audience's interpretation of the message.

- **Word Choice**—the words the writer uses to convey the message.

- **Sentence Fluency**—the flow and rhythm of the writing.

- **Conventions**—the correctness of the grammar, spelling, mechanics, and usage.

- **Presentation**—the appearance of the writing.

The Writing Workshop

Since writing is an involved process that students accomplish at varying speeds, it is usually a good idea to set aside a block of time for them to work on their writing. One time-tested model that has worked well in classrooms is the Writing Workshop. In this model during a set period of time, students work individually and collaboratively (with classmates and/or with the teacher) on different writing activities. One of these activities is for students to collaborate in reviewing each other's manuscripts. One effective technique used in many workshops as a way for students to comment on aspects of each other's writing is to use the language of the traits when they comment.

Some tasks are started and finished during a workshop, while others are ongoing. A writing workshop can serve many writing-related functions:

- Students can work on a class writing assignment (ongoing or quickly accomplished).

- Students can engage in independent writing, jotting down or consulting ideas in their writing log or journal, starting or working on pieces of their own devising.

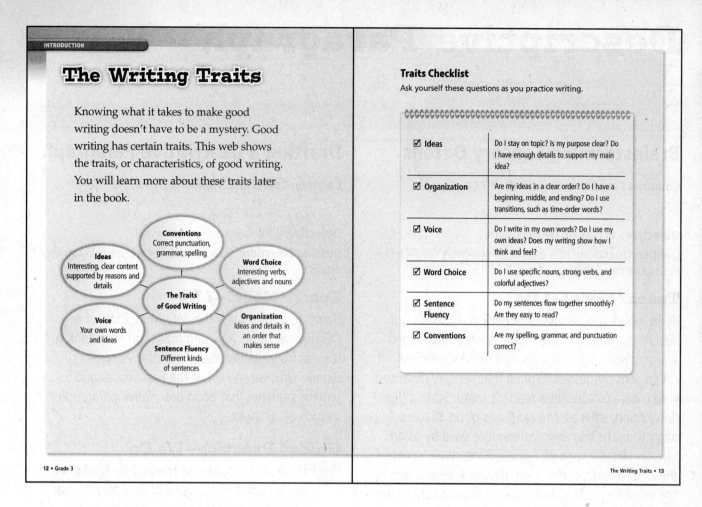

The Writing Traits

Knowing what it takes to make good writing doesn't have to be a mystery. Good writing has certain traits. This web shows the traits, or characteristics, of good writing. You will learn more about these traits later in the book.

Conventions
Correct punctuation, grammar, spelling

Word Choice
Interesting verbs, adjectives and nouns

Ideas
Interesting, clear content supported by reasons and details

The Traits of Good Writing

Voice
Your own words and ideas

Organization
Ideas and details in an order that makes sense

Sentence Fluency
Different kinds of sentences

Traits Checklist

Ask yourself these questions as you practice writing.

☑ Ideas	Do I stay on topic? Is my purpose clear? Do I have enough details to support my main idea?
☑ Organization	Are my ideas in a clear order? Do I have a beginning, middle, and ending? Do I use transitions, such as time-order words?
☑ Voice	Do I write in my own words? Do I use my own ideas? Does my writing show how I think and feel?
☑ Word Choice	Do I use specific nouns, strong verbs, and colorful adjectives?
☑ Sentence Fluency	Do my sentences flow together smoothly? Are they easy to read?
☑ Conventions	Are my spelling, grammar, and punctuation correct?

- As previously mentioned, students can engage in peer-conferencing, giving one another advice about a piece of writing or sharing writing ideas.

- Students can select pieces for inclusion in their writing portfolio, where they keep their best work.

- Teachers can conference with individual students, reviewing student writing and discussing a given student's strengths and weaknesses as well as instructional progress.

- Teachers can engage in small-group instruction with students who need extra help with practice in specific areas of writing.

Writing Workshops are often most effective when they adhere to a dependable schedule and follow a set of clearly posted guidelines (for example, keep voices down, point out the good things about someone's writing as well as comment on aspects that might be revised, listen politely, put away materials when the workshop is over). In addition, students should know what areas of the classroom they can use during the Workshop and should have free access to writing materials, including their handbooks.

You may want to refer to the Writing Workshop pages in this *Common Core Writing Handbook Teacher's Guide* and teach one or two minilessons on writing workshop behaviors and activities so that students have a solid understanding of what is expected of them.

Introduce the Traits

Share the Writing Traits overview pages with students. Discuss each trait briefly and explain to students that their handbooks contain more information on the traits, which they can use to help them as they plan, draft, revise, edit, and publish their writing. Guide students to use their tables of contents or indexes to locate where additional information can be found in their handbooks.

Descriptive Paragraph

Minilesson 1

Brainstorming Sensory Details

Common Core State Standard: W.3.2a

Objective: Brainstorm sensory details.

Guiding Question: How can I think of sensory details for my descriptive paragraph?

Teach/Model—I Do

Read aloud and discuss handbook p. 14. Point out descriptive words in the model, such as *sweet* and *warm, chewy.* Tell students that these words are called sensory details. Explain that sensory details help create pictures in a reader's mind. State a bland description, such as *The cake was good.* Discuss ways to make this description more vivid by using sensory details, such as *I smelled the sweet scent of the cake baking in the oven. I heard the loud ring of the oven timer. The chocolate frosting felt sticky on my fingers. We covered the cake in rainbow-colored sprinkles. The cake tasted like vanilla.* Point out that all five senses are used.

Guided Practice—We Do

Guide students to write sensory details that describe the classroom. Guide students to use all five senses by helping them to complete the following sentences: *I see _____. I hear _____. I taste _____. I smell _____. I touch _____.*

Practice/Apply—You Do

COLLABORATIVE Tell partners to write a description of their favorite place, such as a playground or park. Have students write sensory details using the sentence frames from the We Do activity above.

INDEPENDENT Have students write descriptions of a place where they had a delicious meal. Their descriptions should include sensory details from all five senses.

Conference/Evaluate

Circulate and help students write their sensory details. Remind them to use all five senses.

Minilesson 2

Drafting a Descriptive Paragraph

Common Core State Standard: W.3.2

Objective: Write a descriptive paragraph.

Guiding Question: How do I describe a place using sensory details?

Teach/Model—I Do

Have students review the definition, Parts of a Descriptive Paragraph, and model on handbook p. 14. Discuss how the boldfaced words give sensory details. Go over the list of The Five Senses and remind students that good descriptive paragraphs include all of them.

Guided Practice—We Do

 Have students turn to Frame 1 on handbook p. 15. Together, choose a place everyone has visited, such as the library. Help students suggest sensory details about the place. Guide them to use the senses listed in parentheses to help them think of details. List ideas on the board. Use the list to elicit sentences from students to complete Frame 1. Have students write in their books as you write on the board.

Practice/Apply—You Do

 COLLABORATIVE Have small groups work together to complete Frame 2 with a description of another place.

 INDEPENDENT Have students read the directions. Tell them to use their prewriting plan from Lesson 1 or to brainstorm new ideas using Graphic Organizer 15.

Conference/Evaluate

Circulate and offer encouragement and help as needed. Evaluate using the rubric on p. 104.

WriteSmart CD-ROM

Description; Topic/Central Idea

- eBook
- WriteSmart
- Interactive Lessons

Descriptive Paragraph

A **descriptive paragraph** tells what something is like. It uses specific words and details to paint a picture of the topic. These words help the reader see, feel, hear, and sometimes smell or taste what is being described.

Parts of a Descriptive Paragraph

- A topic sentence that introduces the main idea
- Exact words and vivid details that tell the reader exactly what the topic is like
- Sensory details that help the reader see, hear, smell, taste, and feel things
- A closing sentence that wraps up the paragraph

Pencils

Topic Sentence
Tells the main idea

Exact Words
Paint a clear picture for the reader

Sensory Details
Explain sights, sounds, smells, tastes, and feelings

Closing Sentence
Wraps up the paragraph

My Nana's house is the best place to dunk cookies and basketballs. As soon as you open the door, you **smell** Nana's **sweet** oatmeal cookies. Inside are dozens of **pictures** of my family. My favorite one is from Nana's trip to Alaska. It's a **photo** of her riding a dog sled! Our next stop is the kitchen. There, we have **warm, chewy** cookies and **ice cold** milk. Behind the house, Nana teaches me how to shoot hoops. She still has a perfect free throw. She never misses! I think all the neighbors can hear her **laugh and cheer** every time she sinks one. She **holds** my hands and helps me aim at the hoop. My **heart races** every time. After dinner, Nana drives me home. I never want to leave her house, but I love getting a ride in her cool old convertible!

The Five Senses
Touch
Taste
Sight
Smell
Sound

14 • Grade 3

Name _____

Follow your teacher's directions to complete Frames 1 and 2.

1 There's no place in the world like _____

_____. As soon as you open the door, _____

(see) _____

_____ *(smell)* _____

_____ *(feel)* _____

_____

_____

2 _____

_____ *(see)*

_____

_____

_____ *(smell)*

_____

_____

3 On a separate sheet of paper, use your prewriting plan to write a description, or make a new plan to write about your favorite outdoor place.

Descriptive Paragraph • 15

✓ Corrective Feedback

IF . . . students are not using strong enough descriptive words and details,

THEN . . . remind them that descriptions should paint a clear word picture for the reader. Have students make five columns on a separate sheet of paper and write one of the five senses at the top of each column. Then in that column, have students write details that appeal to that particular sense.

Focus Trait: Word Choice

Explain that choosing exact words helps give the reader a clear picture of the topic being described. On the board, write:

We saw the animals.

Ask students to replace the words *we* and *animals* with more exact words and phrases. Write the improved sentence on the board.

Example: *Elena, Mrs. Gomez, and I saw the tiny brown otters.*

Then write several vague adjectives on the board, such as *hot, fun,* and *pretty.* Have students brainstorm or use a thesaurus to find exact words to replace these.

Examples: *scorching, exciting, gorgeous*

Dialogue

Minilesson 3

Using Natural Speech in Dialogue

Common Core State Standards: W.3.3a, W.3.3b

Objective: Use natural speech in dialogue.

Guiding Question: How do I make speech in dialogue sound natural?

Teach/Model—I Do

Read aloud handbook p. 16. Point out dialogue in the model, noting which person is speaking. Explain that writers add dialogue to help tell the events of the story and to help readers get to know the characters. They choose words that sound like what each character might actually say as statements, questions, and exclamations. Point out that dialogue in the model lets readers know how the narrator feels about the events and sounds like something a young person might say. Point to examples, such as "*That would be the most exciting week ever!*"

Guided Practice—We Do

Ask students what they might say if they were surprised, excited, angry, or scared. Write their ideas on the board in the form of dialogue. Continue guiding students to suggest examples of natural speech until you have a list of at least five sentences.

Practice/Apply—You Do

COLLABORATIVE On the board, write several familiar situations, such as opening a gift, being proud of an accomplishment, or feeling nervous about doing something new. Have small groups choose an event and work together to write natural-sounding dialogue for the situation.

INDEPENDENT Have students choose a different event from the list and write dialogue about it.

Conference/Evaluate

Circulate and help students come up with dialogue that sounds like natural speech. Encourage them to ask themselves, *What would I say in this situation?*

Minilesson 4

Drafting Dialogue

Common Core State Standards: W.3.3a, W.3.3b

Objective: Write dialogue.

Guiding Question: How do I write dialogue?

Teach/Model—I Do

With students, review handbook p. 16. Choose a line of dialogue in the model and point out the quotation marks, the speaker, and the comma that separates the speaker's name from his or her words. Also point out that a new paragraph begins each time someone new starts speaking. Draw students' attention to details that show the characters' feelings, such as *I can't wait to go back to court.*

Guided Practice—We Do

 Have students turn to the frame on handbook p. 17. Guide them to suggest topics and then one to work on together. Help students suggest a sequence of events and dialogue about the topic. Write their suggestions on the board. Then work together to complete the frame. Have students write in their books as you write on the board.

Practice/Apply—You Do

 COLLABORATIVE Ask groups to plan and complete Activity 2. Have them read the dialogue aloud to make sure it sounds like natural speech.

 INDEPENDENT Have students read directions for Activity 3. Tell them to use their prewriting plan from Lesson 2 or to brainstorm new ideas using Graphic Organizer 4.

Conference/Evaluate

During the writing process, circulate and help students create natural-sounding dialogue. Evaluate using the rubric on p. 104.

- eBook
- WriteSmart
- Interactive Lessons

Dialogue

Dialogue is the words spoken by characters. These words help tell the story and share the thoughts and feelings of the characters.

Parts of Dialogue

- The names of the characters who are speaking
- Interesting details that show the thoughts of the characters and help to tell the story
- Quotation marks

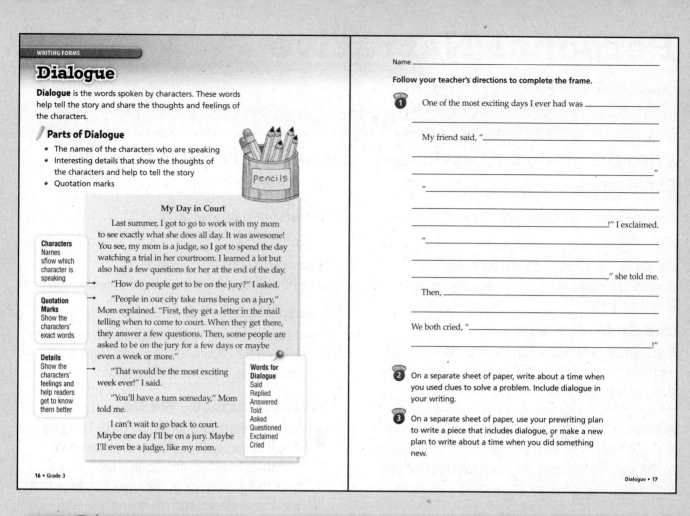

My Day in Court

Last summer, I got to go to work with my mom to see exactly what she does all day. It was awesome! You see, my mom is a judge, so I got to spend the day watching a trial in her courtroom. I learned a lot but also had a few questions for her at the end of the day.

Characters
Names show which character is speaking

"How do people get to be on the jury?" I asked.

Quotation Marks
Show the characters' exact words

"People in our city take turns being on a jury," Mom explained. "First, they get a letter in the mail telling when to come to court. When they get there, they answer a few questions. Then, some people are asked to be on the jury for a few days or maybe even a week or more."

Details
Show the characters' feelings and help readers get to know them better

"That would be the most exciting week ever!" I said.

Words for Dialogue
Said
Replied
Answered
Told
Asked
Questioned
Exclaimed
Cried

"You'll have a turn someday," Mom told me.

I can't wait to go back to court. Maybe one day I'll be on a jury. Maybe I'll even be a judge, like my mom.

Name _____

Follow your teacher's directions to complete the frame.

 1 One of the most exciting days I ever had was _____
_____

My friend said, "_____
_____
_____"

"_____
_____
_____!" I exclaimed.

"_____
_____
_____," she told me.

Then, _____
_____

We both cried, "_____
_____!"

2 On a separate sheet of paper, write about a time when you used clues to solve a problem. Include dialogue in your writing.

3 On a separate sheet of paper, use your prewriting plan to write a piece that includes dialogue, or make a new plan to write about a time when you did something new.

✓ Corrective Feedback

IF . . . students are having trouble adding natural-sounding dialogue,

THEN . . . have them think about the person who is speaking and ask themselves questions such as, *What kinds of words would this person use? Would he or she use formal or informal language? What words would show the speaker's thoughts and feelings? Would he or she use exclamations or ask questions?* Encourage students to use these ideas to write natural-sounding dialogue.

Focus Trait: Word Choice

Remind students that when they write, they should think about the purpose of the piece and what would be interesting to the reader. Since the purpose of a narrative is to tell a story, the dialogue should help tell the events, help readers get to know the characters, and keep readers entertained. Write:

I was bored, so mom said we could go to the park. Then I was happy.

Rewrite the sentences as dialogue with words that would be more interesting to readers.

Example:

"I'm bored," I whined.

"Well, why don't we go to the park?" asked Mom.
"That would be awesome!" I exclaimed.

Personal Narrative

Minilesson 5

Using Description to Develop an Experience

Common Core State Standards: W.3.3, W.3.3a

Objective: Use description to develop an experience.

Guiding Question: How can I use description to help me tell about my experiences?

Teach/Model—I Do

Read aloud and discuss handbook p. 18. Point out words in the model, such as *worried* and *panicked*, that tell how the writer felt. Explain that these thinking and feeling words describe the writer's experience. Also, note that the last sentence shows that the writer's feelings changed from the beginning to the end. Tell students that such descriptions help to develop an experience, or describe it in depth.

Guided Practice—We Do

Guide students to name times when something in their life changed, such as moving to a new place or learning to ride a bike. Write topics on the board as students suggest them, and elicit and write sample sentences with feeling words to go with each topic, making sure the words describe a change of feelings over time. For example: *moving—worried, scared, excited.*

Practice/Apply—You Do

COLLABORATIVE Tell small groups to choose one topic from the list and to brainstorm additional sentences that tell what they feel about that topic.

INDEPENDENT Instruct students to choose a different topic from the board or to come up with a new topic. Then tell them to write two complete sentences that tell their thoughts or feelings about the topic and how they changed over time.

Conference/Evaluate

Circulate and help students find thinking and feeling words for their sentences. You may want to encourage them to use a thesaurus. Completed sentences should reflect how feelings changed over time.

Minilesson 6

Drafting a Personal Narrative

Common Core State Standards: W.3.3, W.3.3d

Objective: Write a personal narrative.

Guiding Question: How do I write a story about myself?

Teach/Model—I Do

Have students review handbook p. 18. Discuss how the boldfaced transitions in the model show time order. Discuss the list of Other Transitions.

Guided Practice—We Do

 Have students turn to handbook p. 19. Explain that it shows writing frames for a personal narrative. Together, decide on a topic about something everyone in the class has done that was initially hard, such as giving a speech. Help students suggest events and feelings about the topic. List their ideas on the board. Use the list to elicit sentences that complete Frame 1 in chronological order. Have students write in their books as you write on the board.

Practice/Apply—You Do

 COLLABORATIVE Have small groups work together to write a narrative for Frame 2 in which they choose and write about another topic. Have groups share what they write.

 INDEPENDENT Have students read the directions. Tell them to use their prewriting plan from Lesson 3 or to brainstorm new ideas using Graphic Organizer 4.

Conference/Evaluate

During the writing process, circulate and offer encouragement and help as needed. Evaluate using the rubric on p. 104.

WriteSmart CD-ROM
Personal Narrative; Transitions

Digital
- eBook
- WriteSmart
- Interactive Lessons

Personal Narrative

A **personal narrative** is a true story about something that happened to the writer. A personal narrative about the writer's life may also be called an autobiography.

✏ Parts of a Personal Narrative

- A beginning that grabs readers' interest
- Events that really happened to the writer, told in time order, or sequence
- Interesting details that elaborate events and the writer's feelings
- Use of the pronoun *I*
- An ending that tells how the story worked out and how the writer felt about it

Beginning
Makes readers want to find out more

Events
Tell what happened in time order

Interesting Details
Include sights, sounds, and feelings

Ending
Wraps up the story and tells how the writer felt

→ When I danced in my first talent show last year, I got a big surprise! It all started when the red curtains opened. Rows of kids sat looking up at me. I stood really still and waited for the music to come on. **At first,** I just worried about messing up my moves. **Then** I had something else to worry about. → The music didn't start! I panicked. I ran off the stage to where Mrs. Meeks had the equipment. The computer battery had died. Suddenly I had an idea. I dug my MP3 player out of my backpack. We plugged it into the → speakers, and my song started blasting! **Finally,** I ran back onstage and danced → like nothing had happened. I guess I did okay, because everyone cheered at the end. Whew, what a close call!

Other Transitions
First
Next
After that
During
After a while
Meanwhile
Later
Last

Name _____

Follow your teacher's directions to complete Frames 1 and 2.

1 One of the hardest things I ever did was _____

_____

At first, _____

_____

_____ . Then _____

_____

_____ . Finally, _____

_____

When it was over, I felt _____

_____

2 _____

_____

_____ . First, _____

_____

_____ . After that, _____

_____

_____ . Finally, _____

_____

3 On a separate sheet of paper, use your prewriting plan to write a personal narrative, or make a new plan to write about something you did that made you proud.

✔ Corrective Feedback

IF . . . students are telling about too many different events in their personal narratives,

THEN . . . remind them that a personal narrative should really be about one main event. Have students write an event, such as *my first time on skis* and jot down details that belong in a description about that event. Then have students cross out any details that don't belong.

✏ Focus Trait: Voice

Remind students that voice should match their purpose. Since their purpose is to tell a story about themselves, they should use a natural-sounding voice and write as if expressing their thoughts and feelings to a friend. Write: *I went to the pool. I was scared to use the diving board for the first time. I jumped, and it was great.*

Have children help you rewrite the sentences in a natural-sounding voice that shows thoughts and feelings.

Example:

I went to the pool. I felt excited yet scared. I was going to jump off the diving board for the first time. As I climbed the ladder, my legs felt shaky. Once I reached the top, I felt terrified, but I really wanted to do it. I held my breath and jumped! I felt free as I flew through the air and splashed into the water. I'm so proud that I overcame my fear.

Person 1 Narrative: Prewriting

Minilesson 7

Determining Audience and Purpose

Common Core State Standards: W.3.3a, W.3.5

Objective: Consider the audience and purpose for writing.

Guiding Question: How do audience and purpose affect my writing?

Teach/Model—I Do

Read and discuss handbook p. 20 with students. Explain that good writers think about their reasons for writing and who their audience will be. They select a topic that will interest their readers and plan to include important events and details that support their topic. Point out the details in the plan on p. 20 (tent falling down, marshmallows catching fire). Explain that unexpected, funny, or interesting details make the audience want to read on.

Guided Practice—We Do

On the board, write several experiences students have shared (*field trip*, *science fair*). Guide them to suppose they are writing a personal narrative to share with another class. Together, select one of the topics and brainstorm important events that support it. List suggestions on the board. Select one of the events and list details about it that would interest the audience.

Practice/Apply—You Do

COLLABORATIVE Have small groups select a different topic from the board and list important events to support it. Have students list interesting details about one event.

INDEPENDENT Have students choose a different important event related to one of the topics and list details about it that would interest their audience.

Conference/Evaluate

Encourage students to ask themselves, *What events best explain the topic to readers? What details would the audience find most interesting and enjoyable?*

Minilesson 8

Planning Clear Event Sequences

Common Core State Standards: W.3.5, W.3.8

Objective: Plan a logical sequence of events.

Guiding Question: How do I choose the best sequence of the events in a personal narrative?

Teach/Model—I Do

With students, review handbook p. 20. Point out that the events in a personal narrative are listed in the order in which they happened. Explain that this keeps readers from being confused and helps them to clearly understand what happened and when. Point out that the order of events in the organizer tells when things happened (*set up tent first, made a fire next, and then slept*).

Guided Practice—We Do

 Direct students to turn to Activity 1 on handbook p. 21. Guide them to suggest events that happened a while ago with someone special. Help students identify three such important events; then work together to list them in order and add interesting details. Have students write in their books as you write on the board.

Practice/Apply—You Do

 COLLABORATIVE Ask students to work in groups to plan and complete Activity 2, making sure to list the events in order.

 INDEPENDENT Have students read the directions for Activity 3. Tell them to use their prewriting plan from Lesson 4 or to brainstorm new ideas using Graphic Organizer 4.

Conference/Evaluate

During the writing process, circulate and help students list events in chronological order. Evaluate using the rubric on p. 104.

Digital
• eBook
• WriteSmart
• Interactive Lessons

Personal Narrative: Prewriting

A **personal narrative** tells a true story about something that happened to the author. Before you write a personal narrative, you should prewrite to brainstorm and plan your ideas.

Prewriting

- First, brainstorm a list of possible topics. For a personal narrative, think about interesting things that have happened to you or things you have done.
- Then, choose an event you would like to share with readers. Use a graphic organizer to plan the interesting details to include.

Topic brainstorming
School talent show
(Backyard campout with Dad)
Flying on an airplane

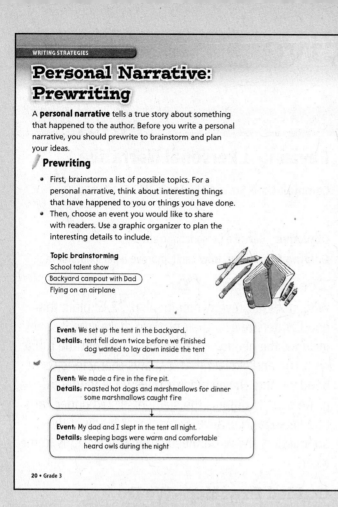

Event: We set up the tent in the backyard.
Details: tent fell down twice before we finished
dog wanted to lay down inside the tent

Event: We made a fire in the fire pit.
Details: roasted hot dogs and marshmallows for dinner
some marshmallows caught fire

Event: My dad and I slept in the tent all night.
Details: sleeping bags were warm and comfortable
heard owls during the night

Name _____

Follow your teacher's directions to complete this page.

1 **Topic:** A time I did something with someone special

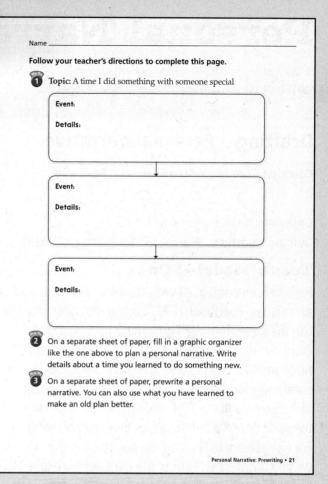

Event:

Details:

Event:

Details:

Event:

Details:

2 On a separate sheet of paper, fill in a graphic organizer like the one above to plan a personal narrative. Write details about a time you learned to do something new.

3 On a separate sheet of paper, prewrite a personal narrative. You can also use what you have learned to make an old plan better.

✔ Corrective Feedback

IF . . . students are having difficulty selecting which events and details to include,

THEN . . . ask what they want the audience to know about the topic. Have students select events that would be the most interesting or entertaining to readers. Then, ask what details would best explain or support these events. Remind them that often the most interesting details are those that are unusual or unexpected.

Focus Trait: Ideas

Remind students that important and interesting details in a personal narrative help readers understand what happened and make them want to read more. Explain that since the audience was not there when the event occurred, details can help paint a clear picture of what took place. Write:

Dad made a fire. We cooked hot dogs and marshmallows.

Then rewrite the sentences to include important and interesting details. Example:

Dad used wood from our fireplace to make a roaring fire in the brick fire pit in our backyard. We stuck hot dogs on the ends of broken-off tree branches and held them over the fire to cook. Then, we put marshmallows on the sticks and held them over the fire until they were toasty brown outside and gooey inside.

Personal Narrative

Minilesson 9

Drafting a Personal Narrative

Common Core State Standards: W.3.3a, W.3.3b

Objective: Draft a personal narrative.

Guiding Question: How do I turn prewriting into a draft?

Teach/Model—I Do

Review handbook p. 20 with students, and then read and discuss handbook p. 22. Explain that good writers use the ideas from their prewriting to draft a story. Point out that the events and details from the organizer are now written with complete sentences in paragraph form, including an interesting beginning, time order words, and an ending. Explain that writers may add or leave out details as they write the draft. For example, details about the dog were in the prewriting but were left out of the draft, while details about Mom that weren't in the prewriting were added.

Guided Practice—We Do

 Direct students to handbook p. 23. Guide them to use the organizer you created on handbook p. 21 to draft a narrative in the frame on p. 23. Add and delete details as needed. Include time order clues. Have students write in their books as you write on the board.

Practice/Apply—You Do

 COLLABORATIVE Have small groups use their prewriting plan from handbook p. 21 to complete Activity 2, making sure to include a beginning, a middle with details and time order clues, and an ending.

 INDEPENDENT Have students complete Activity 3 using their prewriting plan from handbook p. 21.

Conference/Evaluate

Remind students that they should use their prewriting plans as a guide but are free to make changes as they draft.

Minilesson 10

Revising a Personal Narrative

Common Core State Standard: W.3.5

Objective: Revise a personal narrative.

Guiding Question: How can I improve a personal narrative?

Teach/Model—I Do

With students, review handbook p. 22. Explain that good writers review their work to make sure it includes the needed components. Point out the rubric on p.104 and explain that it shows characteristics of good writing. Have students review the model to make sure it contains the elements listed under Parts of a Personal Narrative. Explain that if any of these are missing, the writer needs to make revisions to the draft.

Guided Practice—We Do

Direct students to their draft on handbook p. 23. Together, identify the characteristics of a personal narrative. Ask questions such as, *What time order clues did we use? Would adding other time order words make the writing clearer? What interesting details did we include? Should we add more? Should we cross off any details that don't fit?* Make revisions on the board as students work in their books.

Practice/Apply—You Do

COLLABORATIVE Ask students to work in pairs to revise their draft from Activity 2. Remind them to refer to the rubric.

INDEPENDENT Have students revise their draft from Activity 3. Remind them to use the rubric.

Conference/Evaluate

During the writing process, circulate and help students improve their writing. Evaluate using the rubric on p. 104.

 Digital
- eBook
- WriteSmart
- Interactive Lessons

Personal Narrative

A **personal narrative** is a story about the writer's experiences. It tells his or her thoughts and feelings.

Parts of a Personal Narrative

- A beginning that gets readers interested
- Time clues that show the order of events
- Details that are grouped together in a way that makes sense
- An ending that tells how the story worked out

Beginning
Catches the readers' interest so they want to keep reading

Details
Tell the events in order and are grouped with other details about the same thing

Time Clues
Help show when events happen or how long they last

Ending
Tells how everything worked out

A Night Under the Stars

Last spring, my dad and I had the most amazing campout ever. The best part was that we never left home. We had a campout in the backyard. As soon as I got home from school, we started to set up the tent. That was kind of tricky. The tent fell down twice before we got it finished. We laughed so hard I almost fell down, too! Once that was done, Dad made a fire. We used some of the wood for our fireplace. We cooked hot dogs on the fire, and then we toasted marshmallows. Mom came out and cooked with us, too. Her marshmallows kept catching fire, so Dad shared with her. When Mom went in the house, Dad and I crawled into the tent. We heard owls hooting, so we decided to tell spooky stories. Finally we fell asleep. We both slept great. It was the perfect campout!

Other Words that Tell Time Order
Before that
Earlier in the day
First
Later
Meanwhile
Soon
When I was younger

Name _____

Follow your teacher's directions to complete this page.

 When I was younger, I got to _____

with _____

First, _____

_____

_____

_____

Later _____

_____

_____

Eventually, _____

_____

_____

The best part was _____

_____

_____

_____

 On a separate sheet of paper, write a personal narrative about a time you learned to do something new.

On a separate sheet of paper, use your prewriting plan to write a personal narrative, or make a new plan to write about your most exciting day.

✔ Corrective Feedback

IF . . . students are having difficulty determining whether or not they have included enough details in the draft,

THEN . . . have them read the draft aloud to a partner. Direct writers to ask their partners for suggestions. Have them ask questions such as *Do you have any questions about my writing? Were any of the ideas unclear to you? What would make the story more interesting or easier to understand?* Encourage writers to revise their drafts accordingly.

✐ Focus Trait: Sentence Fluency

Remind students that time order clues help readers understand the order of the events in the story, show when the events happened, and explain how long the events lasted. Write:

I learned to ride my bike. I had a tricycle. I ride my bike with my dad every weekend.

Explain that time order clues would help to make the sentences flow more naturally and tell when each of the events happened.

Then rewrite the sentences to include time order clues.

Example:

When I was five years old, I learned to ride my bike. Before that, I had a tricycle. Now, I ride my bike with my dad every weekend.

Response Paragraph

Minilesson 11

Summarizing

Common Core State Standards: W.3.2, W.3.4

Objective: Select key points to include in a summary.
Guiding Question: For a summary, how do I choose the ideas that are most important?

Teach/Model—I Do
Read aloud and discuss handbook p. 24. Point out details in the model that tell what happened in *Goldilocks: A Modern Tale.* Explain that, for the summary part of the response, the writer did not retell the entire story but included only the most important events and details. Explain that summarizing means choosing the most important details and events and writing them in your own words. Model how to summarize by telling the key events from another familiar story.

Guided Practice—We Do
Have students name stories that everyone is familiar with, such as ones you've read in class. Write at least five titles on the board as students suggest them. Then work together to list three or four events for a summary of one of the stories. Encourage students to think about which events are the most important. List them on the board, emphasizing that you are retelling in your own words.

Practice/Apply—You Do
COLLABORATIVE Tell small groups to choose another title from the list. Instruct them to work together to list the most important events for a summary.

INDEPENDENT Instruct students to choose a different title from the board or to come up with a new title. Then tell them to write three events they would include in a summary of the story.

Conference/Evaluate
Circulate and help students summarize. Elicit the story's problem, a key event, and the resolution.

Minilesson 12

Drafting a Response Paragraph

Common Core State Standards: W.3.1, W.3.4

Objective: Write a response to literature.
Guiding Question: How do I tell my opinion about a story?

Teach/Model—I Do
Have students review handbook p. 24. Discuss how the boldfaced transitions in the model show time order. Go over the list of Other Transitions. Point out that the last sentence gives an opinion.

Guided Practice—We Do
 Have students turn to the frame on handbook p. 25. Mention that the transitions will help you write in time order. Name a story the entire class has read, and have students tell what they think about the story. Use their suggestions to write a topic sentence. Then guide them to suggest important events and details from the story. List their ideas and use the list to create sentences to complete the frame. Have students write in their books as you write on the board.

Practice/Apply—You Do
 COLLABORATIVE Have small groups work together to write a response to another story. Encourage them to tell about only the events that support their main idea.

 INDEPENDENT Have students read the directions. Tell them to use their prewriting plan from Lesson 6 or to brainstorm new ideas using Graphic Organizer 7.

Conference/Evaluate
During the writing process, circulate and offer encouragement and help as needed. Evaluate using the rubric on p. 104.

WriteSmart CD-ROM
Response to Literature

Digital
• eBook
• WriteSmart
• Interactive Lessons

Response Paragraph

A **response paragraph** is writing that tells about what you have read and what you think about it.

Parts of a Response Paragraph

- An interesting opening
- A topic sentence that mentions the title
- Details and examples that tell something about the selection. For a story, they tell about the characters or what happens.
- The writer's thoughts, feelings, and ideas about the selection

Topic Sentence Includes the title

Details and Examples Tell about the selection

Writer's thoughts and feelings

Transitions Show time order or link ideas

Have your parents ever said you are too picky? Well, I would tell you and them to read <u>Goldilocks: A Modern Tale</u>. In that story, Goldie is just too hard to please. **To start with**, Goldie becomes a judge on a cooking show. She tastes three kinds of pizza. She says Dad Bear's pizza is icky because it has too much sauce. **Then** she dislikes the cheese on Mom Bear's pizza. When she tastes Kid Bear's peanut butter pizza she says, "Hmm. This is pretty odd." **Later**, she wins a trip to the mountains. The bears loan her some skis. I thought she would be happy, but she was not. She says they are the wrong color! She does not even say "Thank you." I could not believe that she was so rude. **In the end**, Goldie learns not to be so picky. She even starts to like peanut butter pizza! I thought <u>Goldilocks: A Modern Tale</u> was a great book!

Other Transitions
First of all
Second
Plus
Another
So
Finally

Name _____

Follow your teacher's directions to complete the frame.

1 In the story _____

_____

_____

To start with, _____

_____

_____ Then _____

_____

_____

_____

Later, _____

_____

_____ In the end, _____

_____

_____

_____

2 On another sheet of paper, write a response paragraph about another book you have read. Remember to give details from the book as well as your feelings about it.

3 On a separate sheet of paper, use your prewriting plan to write a response paragraph, or make a new plan to write about how another character changed during a story.

✔ Corrective Feedback

IF . . . students are still having trouble placing quotation marks correctly,

THEN . . . remind them that quotation marks go around the speaker's exact words. Explain that, when they are using the words of an author, the quotation marks are placed before the first word that came directly from the story and after the final word that came directly from the story. If the words from the story are restated or summarized, quotation marks are not needed.

Focus Trait: Ideas

Explain to students that not every detail from the story will support their main idea. Even if an event is very important to the plot of the story, it might not support the main idea of the response paragraph.

Review the student model on handbook p. 24. Have students identify the main idea and some details that support it. Then, on the board, write several new sentences about the story, such as:

When she was a baby, Goldie didn't like any of the bibs her parents bought her. The bears come home from vacation, and their door is wide open. Kid Bear helps Goldie realize she's being too picky.

Then discuss why each detail does or does not support the main idea of the response paragraph.

Opinion Paragraph

Minilesson 13

Writing an Opinion Statement

Common Core State Standard: W.3.1a

Objective: Write an opinion statement that can be supported by reasons.

Guiding Question: How do I write an opinion statement that I can support?

Teach/Model—I Do

Read aloud handbook p. 26. Remind students that an opinion is a person's thoughts or viewpoint. Point out that the first sentence in the model clearly states the writer's opinion about the topic. Explain that writers should give an opinion statement that they will be able to support with reasons, information, or examples. Point out the reasons in the model that support the writer's point of view, such as *Who ever really gets to trade a cow for magic beans?*

Guided Practice—We Do

On the board, write five topics that would be familiar to students, such as story titles, sports, or school activities. Together, select a topic and then guide students to suggest opinion statements about it. Write their suggestions on the board. As you write, guide students to suggest reasons to support their opinions.

Practice/Apply—You Do

COLLABORATIVE Have small groups select another topic from the board and write an opinion statement about it. Tell students to discuss possible reasons that would support the opinion.

INDEPENDENT Have students select a different topic from the list and write an opinion statement about it. Have them list two reasons to support the opinion.

Conference/Evaluate

Remind students of the difference between facts and opinions. Guide them to write an opinion statement that tells their point of view about the topic. Ask, *How do you feel about that? What do you think?*

Minilesson 14

Drafting an Opinion Paragraph

Common Core State Standards: W.3.1a, W.3.1b

Objective: Write an opinion paragraph.

Guiding Question: How do I write an opinion paragraph that explains my point of view?

Teach/Model—I Do

With students, review handbook p. 26. Point out the opinion statement, supporting reasons, and examples. Also point out that linking words such as *because* and *since* connect the reasons to the opinion, and explain that the conclusion reminds readers of the opinion.

Guided Practice—We Do

 Direct students to the frame on handbook p. 27. Help them suggest familiar books or stories, and choose one together. Help students write an opinion statement about the book and suggest reasons and examples to support their point of view. Write their suggestions on the board. Then work together to complete the frame with the opinion statement and reasons. Have students write in their books as you write on the board.

Practice/Apply—You Do

 COLLABORATIVE Have students work in pairs to plan and complete Activity 2. Have pairs share their opinion paragraphs.

INDEPENDENT Have students read the directions for Activity 3. Tell them to use their prewriting plan from Lesson 7 or to brainstorm new ideas using Graphic Organizer 7.

Conference/Evaluate

During the writing process, circulate and help students create opinion statements that they can strongly support. Evaluate using the rubric on p. 104.

 Digital ▸
- eBook
- WriteSmart
- Interactive Lessons

Opinion Paragraph

An **opinion paragraph** tells what the writer thinks about a topic. It explains why he or she has this view.

Parts of an Opinion Paragraph

- A topic sentence that introduces the writer's opinion
- Reasons that support the point of view
- Linking words that connect the opinion to reasons
- A concluding statement that ties ideas together

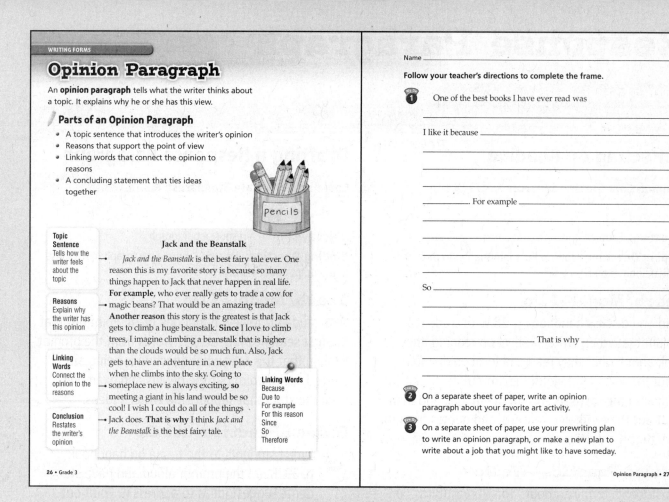

Topic Sentence
Tells how the writer feels about the topic

Reasons
Explain why the writer has this opinion

Linking Words
Connect the opinion to the reasons

Conclusion
Restates the writer's opinion

Jack and the Beanstalk

Jack and the Beanstalk is the best fairy tale ever. One reason this is my favorite story is because so many things happen to Jack that never happen in real life. **For example**, who ever really gets to trade a cow for magic beans? That would be an amazing trade! **Another reason** this story is the greatest is that Jack gets to climb a huge beanstalk. **Since** I love to climb trees, I imagine climbing a beanstalk that is higher than the clouds would be so much fun. Also, Jack gets to have an adventure in a new place when he climbs into the sky. Going to someplace new is always exciting, **so** meeting a giant in his land would be so cool! I wish I could do all of the things Jack does. **That is why** I think *Jack and the Beanstalk* is the best fairy tale.

Linking Words
Because
Due to
For example
For this reason
Since
So
Therefore

Name _____

Follow your teacher's directions to complete the frame.

 1 One of the best books I have ever read was

_____

I like it because _____

_____

_____

_____

_____ . For example _____

_____

_____

So _____

_____

_____ . That is why _____

_____

_____

 2 On a separate sheet of paper, write an opinion paragraph about your favorite art activity.

3 On a separate sheet of paper, use your prewriting plan to write an opinion paragraph, or make a new plan to write about a job that you might like to have someday.

✓ Corrective Feedback

IF . . . students are having trouble supporting their opinion statement,

THEN . . . have them brainstorm a list of reasons why they hold this point of view and select the three that most strongly support the opinion. If they continue to struggle, encourage them to restate the opinion in a way that can more easily be supported. For example, if students are having difficulty supporting a statement such as *Reading is fun*, have them change the statement to *Reading is important*.

Focus Trait: Organization

Remind students that a topic sentence is found at the beginning of an opinion paragraph and lets readers know what the paragraph will be about. When writing an opinion paragraph, the topic sentence introduces the writer's beliefs and feelings about the topic. Explain that a strong topic sentence clearly states the writer's point of view. Write:

We play soccer.

Explain that this tells readers that the topic of the paragraph is soccer but does not introduce the writer's opinion about the sport. Write:

Being part of a soccer team is a great experience.

Point out that this introduces the topic, lets readers know how the writer feels, and can be supported with reasons and examples.

Response Paragraph

Minilesson 15

Reflecting on Reading

Common Core State Standards: W.3.1a, W.3.1b

Objective: Form an opinion about a text.

Guiding Question: How do I use information to form an opinion about a text?

Teach/Model—I Do

Read and discuss handbook p. 28 with students. Explain that when writers reflect on reading, they think about what they read and form an opinion about the text. Read aloud the prompt. Point out the opinion in the first sentence of the model, and then point out the examples, reasons, and quotes from the story that the writer used as a basis for the opinion.

Guided Practice—We Do

Ask students to think about "The Harvest Birds" or another short story. On the board, write *Why do you think Grandpa Chon agreed to help Juan?* Guide students to suggest opinions to answer the prompt. Have students identify information from the story to support their opinions, such as *I think Grandpa Chon let Juan use the land because he thought Juan might be able to teach him a different way to grow crops. He asked Juan to tell him his secret at the end of the story.* Write students' suggestions on the board.

Practice/Apply—You Do

COLLABORATIVE Have students suggest several familiar stories. On the board, write *With which character do you have the most in common?* Have small groups choose a character from one of the stories and work together to write an opinion about the prompt, including a detail or example to support it.

INDEPENDENT Have students choose a different character from a story on the list and answer the same prompt, including support for the opinion.

Conference/Evaluate

Encourage students to ask themselves, *What part of the story caused me to have this opinion?*

Minilesson 16

Drafting a Response Paragraph

Common Core State Standards: W.3.1a, W.3.1b

Objective: Write a response paragraph.

Guiding Question: How do I write a paragraph in response to a prompt about a story?

Teach/Model—I Do

With students, review handbook p. 28. Point out that the first sentence repeats key words from the prompt. Explain that this tells what question is being answered. Next, point out the details and examples from the story that support the writer's ideas.

Guided Practice—We Do

 Direct students to the frame on handbook p. 29. Read the prompt aloud and have students suggest ideas to address it. Point out that the beginning of the frame restates a portion of the prompt. Guide students to complete the first sentence. Help them identify details and examples from the story to support their ideas, and list their suggestions on the board. Then, work together to complete the frame. Have students write in their books as you write on the board.

Practice/Apply—You Do

 COLLABORATIVE Ask students to work in groups to plan and complete Activity 2. Have students read and discuss their response paragraphs.

 INDEPENDENT Have students read the directions for Activity 3. Tell them to use their prewriting plan from Lesson 8 or to brainstorm new ideas using Graphic Organizer 7.

Conference/Evaluate

During the writing process, circulate and help students identify details to explain their ideas. Evaluate using the rubric on p. 104.

Digital
• eBook
• WriteSmart
• Interactive Lessons

Response Paragraph

A **response paragraph** tells the writer's answer to a question or a prompt. Sometimes, the response answers a question about a story.

Parts of a Response Paragraph

- A topic sentence that uses words from the prompt
- Details and examples that explain the writer's ideas
- Quotation marks that go around a speaker's exact words

pencils

Topic Sentence
Words from the prompt show what question is being answered

Details and Examples
Explain the writer's ideas

Quotation Marks
Show any exact words from the story

The Harvest Birds

Prompt: How do you think the people in town felt about Juan at the end of the story?

At the end of the story, I think the townspeople started to feel respect for Juan. One thing that shows this is when the story says, "When Juan arrived in town, everyone was amazed." They saw that he was a great farmer because he had such a wonderful harvest. They were surprised he was able to grow so much food. Next, some of them even asked for his advice. They said, "Teach me your secrets!" Some other people even offered to give him a job. They were not laughing at him now. They respected him and wanted him to work for them.

Other Transitions
First
Then
After that
During
After a while
Later
Last
Finally

Name _____

Follow your teacher's directions to complete the frame.

 1 Prompt: Why do you think Juan had such a great harvest?

I think Juan had a great harvest because _____
_____

At first, _____
_____
_____

_____ Then, _____
_____
_____

_____. In the story, it says, "_____
_____
_____"

Last, _____
_____
_____

2 On a separate sheet of paper, write a response paragraph to answer the following: What do you think would be the best part of working as an illustrator?

3 On a separate sheet of paper, use your prewriting plan to write a response paragraph, or make a new plan to answer the following prompt: Why are pictures important to a story?

✔ Corrective Feedback

IF . . . students are having trouble identifying facts and examples to explain their ideas,

THEN . . . have them reread their topic sentence. Ask, *What happened in the story that caused you to have this opinion or idea?* Guide students to look back through the story to find these events or examples.

Focus Trait: Word Choice

Remind students that linking words help to connect ideas in writing. Explain that when writing a response paragraph, writers should connect their opinions with the supporting reasons, details, and examples. Linking words such as *because, therefore, since,* and *for example* can be used to connect these ideas. Write:

Cinderella would make a great princess. She was nice to everyone.

Then rewrite the sentences using linking words. Explain that linking words connect ideas and show how they relate to one another.

Example: *Cinderella would make a great princess because she was nice to everyone. For example, she was even friends with the mice and birds.*

Response to Literature: Prewriting

Minilesson 17

Planning a Response

Common Core State Standards: W.3.1a, W.3.1b, W.3.5

Objective: Plan a response to a prompt.

Guiding Question: How do I plan a response?

Teach/Model—I Do

Read and discuss handbook p. 30 with students. Explain that a response to literature begins with an opinion statement that also repeats words from the prompt. The writer then lists details from the story to support the opinion. Explain that some details may be quotes (*"Even though…"*). Tell students that good writers organize their ideas and plan the response before beginning to write. They select the reasons and details that best support their opinion.

Guided Practice—We Do

Select a familiar story, such as *Goldilocks*. Write the prompt: *Do you think the main character was a good role model?* Discuss students' ideas and guide them to select the most popular opinion. Guide students to develop an opinion statement. Write it on the board in an organizer similar to the one in the handbook. Have students suggest reasons and details to support the opinion. Elicit responses such as *She was not a good role model because she went in their house without permission.* Write their ideas on the board.

Practice/Apply—You Do

COLLABORATIVE Have small groups select a different familiar story and complete an organizer to address the same prompt.

INDEPENDENT Have students choose a new story and complete an organizer to address the prompt.

Conference/Evaluate

Encourage students to write an opinion statement that can be supported with details from the story. Ask *What happened to cause you to have this opinion? What words or actions of the character support your opinion?*

Minilesson 18

Citing Examples from the Text

Common Core State Standard: W.3.1b

Objective: Choose effective supporting details.

Guiding Question: How do I select details and examples?

Teach/Model—I Do

Review handbook p. 30 with students. Point out that the details are examples that the author cites from the story to support the reasons and opinion. Show how each detail supports the opinion statement. Only examples that strongly support the opinion should be included in the organizer.

Guided Practice—We Do

 1 Direct students to handbook p. 31 and read aloud the prompt about *Max's Words*. Have students suggest opinions and write them on the board. Have them consider which can be supported by the text. Together, choose an opinion. Guide students to suggest reasons and strong supporting examples, including quotes. Help students identify the three examples from the text that most strongly support the opinion. Have students write in their books as you write on the board.

Practice/Apply—You Do

 2 **COLLABORATIVE** Ask students to work in groups to plan and complete Activity 2, making sure to include the strongest examples.

 3 **INDEPENDENT** Have students read the directions for Activity 3. Tell them to use their prewriting plan from Lesson 9 or to brainstorm new ideas using Graphic Organizer 7.

Conference/Evaluate

During the writing process, circulate and help students select strong examples. Evaluate using the rubric on p. 104.

 Digital
- eBook
- WriteSmart
- Interactive Lessons

Response to Literature: Prewriting

A **response to literature** answers a prompt or question about a story.

Prewriting

- Begin by listing your ideas about the prompt.
- Then, choose which idea to write about. Use a graphic organizer to plan the details, examples, and quotes to use in your response.

Prompt: Why do you think Jiichan wanted to be the kamishibai man again?

Topic brainstorming
He enjoyed riding his bike to the city
He hoped to see the grown-up kids again
(He liked being around the kids)

> **Opinion:** I think Jiichan wanted to be the kamishibai man again because he liked being with kids.
>
> **Reason:** He must like kids because he and his wife called each other Grandma and Grandpa.
> **Details:** "Even though they never had children of their own, they called each other 'Jiichan' and 'Baachan'. Jiichan is Grandpa, and Baachan is Grandma."
>
> **Reason:** He was excited to go back to the city to see the kids.
> **Details:** hummed a tune as he rode his bike to town
>
> **Reason:** He called the kids and gave them candy when they came to hear the stories.
> **Details:** yelled and used clappers to get their attention; knew which candy they liked best

---

Name _____

Follow your teacher's directions to complete this page.

1 **Prompt:** How do you think Max felt about his collection in *Max's Words?*

Opinion:
Reason:
Details:
Reason:
Details:
Reason:
Details:

2 On a separate sheet of paper, fill in a graphic organizer like the one above. Write your ideas for a response to literature for the following prompt: What would you most enjoy about someone like the kamishibai man? Think about reasons and details to support your opinion.

3 On a separate sheet of paper, prewrite a response to literature. You can also use what you have learned to make an old plan better.

✔ Corrective Feedback

IF . . . students are having difficulty selecting which examples to include,

THEN . . . have them complete an idea web, such as Graphic Organizer 15, and include any examples, details, or quotes that support their opinion statement. Next, have them put a star by the strongest example, then by the second strongest example, and so on until they have selected the best ones to include in the response.

Focus Trait: Organization

Remind students that a response to literature begins with an opinion statement that tells the writer's ideas about the prompt. This opinion statement should be something that can be supported with reasons, details, and examples from the text. It should also clearly identify the writer's point of view. Write:

I read about what happened when Goldilocks met the bear family.

Point out that this sentence does not tell the writer's opinion. It also would be difficult to prove this statement using examples from the text. Have students suggest effective opinion statements, and write their suggestions on the board. Example:

I do not believe Goldilocks is a good role model because she did things in the bears' home that they did not want her to do.

Response to Literature

Minilesson 19

Drafting a Response to Literature

Common Core State Standards: W.3.1a, W.3.1b

Objective: Draft a response to literature.

Guiding Question: How do I draft a response to literature?

Teach/Model—I Do

Review handbook p. 30 with students, pointing out the prompt, opinion, reasons, and details. Then read and discuss handbook p. 32, explaining that the writer used the ideas from the organizer to draft the response and included linking words such as *because* and *also* to connect details to the opinion. Explain that writers may add details (*Only someone who liked the kids would learn what candy is their favorite*) or leave other details out (*Yelled and used clappers*) to improve the story as they write the draft. Also point out that the conclusion reminds readers of the opinion and wraps up the ideas.

Guided Practice—We Do

 With students, read aloud the prompt on handbook p. 33. Together, use their prewriting plan from Lesson 9 to complete the frame. Guide students to add and delete details as needed. Include linking words and a conclusion. Have students write in their books as you write on the board.

Practice/Apply—You Do

 COLLABORATIVE Have small groups plan and complete Activity 2, making sure to include linking words, a conclusion, and ideas from the organizer they created during Lesson 9, Activity 2.

 INDEPENDENT Ask students to complete Activity 3 using their prewriting plan from Lesson 9 or to plan and draft a response to the prompt in the handbook.

Conference/Evaluate

Remind students that writing in complete sentences and adding linking words helps transform ideas from prewriting into a draft.

Minilesson 20

Revising a Response to Literature

Common Core State Standard: W.3.5

Objective: Revise a response to literature.

Guiding Question: How do I revise a response to literature to strengthen my writing?

Teach/Model—I Do

With students, review handbook p. 32. Explain that good writers review a response to literature to make sure it answers the prompt, repeats words from the question in the opening, includes details and examples, includes linking words, has a conclusion, and uses quotation marks around exact words from the story. Point out the rubric on p. 104; explain that it shows characteristics of good writing. Have students review the model and look for the parts of a response. Explain that if any of these were missing, the writer would need to make changes to the draft.

Guided Practice—We Do

Direct students to their drafts on handbook p. 33. Together, identify the characteristics of a response to literature. Ask questions such as, *What linking words connect the ideas? Are any ideas repeated? Do details and examples support the opinion?* Make revisions on the board as students work in their books.

Practice/Apply—You Do

COLLABORATIVE Ask students to work in groups to revise their draft from Activity 2. Remind them to refer to the rubric on p. 104.

INDEPENDENT Have students revise their draft from Activity 3. Remind them to use the rubric.

Conference/Evaluate

During the writing process, circulate and help students improve their writing. Evaluate using the rubric on p. 104.

 Digital
- eBook
- WriteSmart
- Interactive Lessons

Response to Literature

A **response to literature** explains the writer's ideas about a story. It answers a question or prompt about the text.

Parts of a Response to Literature

- A topic sentence that includes some words from the prompt and tells the writer's opinion
- Details and examples that support the writer's ideas
- Exact words from the story in quotation marks
- Linking words that connect the opinion and details
- A clear conclusion that wraps up the ideas

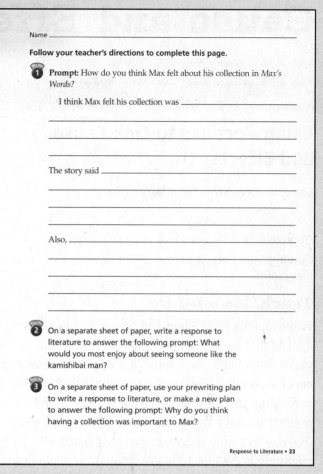

Topic Sentence
Repeats words from the prompt and tells the main idea

Linking Words
Connect the writer's opinion to the supporting details

Details
Support the opinion

Conclusion
Wraps up the ideas

Prompt: Why do you think Jiichan wanted to be the kamishibai man again?

I think Jiichan wanted to be the kamishibai man again because he enjoyed being with the kids. He must have liked kids, since he and his wife called each other Grandma and Grandpa. The story said, "Even though they never had children of their own, they called each other 'Jiichan' and 'Baachan,'" which mean Grandma and Grandpa. He was so excited to see the kids that he hummed a tune as he rode his bike to town. He also gave the kids their favorite candy. Only someone who really likes kids would learn what candy is their favorite. Jiichan wanted to be the kamishibai man again because he wanted to be with the kids again.

Other Linking Words
Because
For example
For this reason
Since
So
Therefore

Follow your teacher's directions to complete this page.

1 **Prompt:** How do you think Max felt about his collection in *Max's Words?*

I think Max felt his collection was _____

_____

_____

_____

The story said _____

_____

_____

_____

Also, _____

_____

_____

_____

_____

2 On a separate sheet of paper, write a response to literature to answer the following prompt: What would you most enjoy about seeing someone like the kamishibai man?

3 On a separate sheet of paper, use your prewriting plan to write a response to literature, or make a new plan to answer the following prompt: Why do you think having a collection was important to Max?

✓ Corrective Feedback

IF . . . students are having difficulty determining how to improve their drafts,

THEN . . . have them work with a partner to use the definition and Parts of a Response to Literature on handbook p. 32, as well as the rubric on p. 104, as checklists. Guide them to work together to look for each attribute in their writing and to make changes accordingly.

Focus Trait: Sentence Fluency

Remind students that each sentence should introduce a new idea. Once an idea has been mentioned, it should not be repeated in the following sentences. Also, once a proper noun has been stated, it should not be repeated in the next sentence. Pronouns should replace proper nouns in following sentences. Write:

The kamishibai man liked the kids. The kamishibai man wanted to see the kids because he liked the kids and missed being with the kids.

Discuss ways to improve the sentences to avoid redundancy. Revise the sentence to improve fluency. Example:

The kamishibai man liked the kids. He wanted to see them because he missed being with them.

Cause and Effect Paragraphs

Minilesson 21

Using *Because* to Link Cause and Effects

Common Core State Standard: W.3.2c

Objective: Use *because* to link cause and effects.

Guiding Question: How can I use *because* to link effects to their cause?

Teach/Model—I Do

With students, read aloud and discuss handbook p. 34. Explain that events can be related. An event that makes something else happen is a cause. The resulting event is an effect. Point out causes and effects in the model that use the word *because*, such as *...birds migrate because days grow shorter in the fall*. Explain that days growing shorter is the cause and birds migrating is the effect. Choose another example from the model and write it on the board, explaining that *because* is always placed in front of the cause.

Guided Practice—We Do

With students, write two effects of reading for pleasure, such as *learning new words* or *enjoying exciting stories*. Guide students to link their cause and effects with because, such as *Because I read for pleasure, I learn new words*. Write students' sentences on the board.

Practice/Apply—You Do

COLLABORATIVE Have pairs work together to list at least two effects of the popularity of the Internet, such as *many people send e-mail instead of land mail*. Have students link their cause and effects with *because*.

INDEPENDENT Have students work independently to list at least two effects of eating healthy foods. Remind students to use the word *because* to link effects to the cause.

Conference/Evaluate

As students work, circulate and help them properly link their causes and effects. Make sure they write full sentences.

Minilesson 22

Drafting Cause and Effect Paragraphs

Common Core State Standards: W.3.2, W.3.7

Objective: Draft cause and effect paragraphs.

Guiding Question: How do I use details to show cause-and-effect relationships?

Teach/Model—I Do

Review the model on handbook p. 34. Tell students that they can find different effects of a cause or different causes for an effect by using different sources. Point to the model and explain that the writer found one source in which scientists say that birds migrate because of cold weather. Another source says that birds migrate because there is less sunlight in the fall.

Guided Practice—We Do

 Direct students to the frame on handbook p. 35. Read the introduction. Help students use classroom resources to find information about dinosaurs. Guide students to identify cause-and-effect relationships, such as *scientists think a giant asteroid hit the Earth, causing a lot of damage to the planet*. Work together to complete the frame. Have students write in their books as you write on the board.

Practice/Apply—You Do

 COLLABORATIVE Have small groups plan and complete Activity 2. Tell groups to carefully read the prompt and then use two sources to find effects of the invention of the airplane.

 INDEPENDENT Have students read and follow the directions.

Conference/Evaluate

As students draft, have them evaluate their work using the rubric on p. 104.

Digital
- eBook
- WriteSmart
- Interactive Lessons

Cause and Effect Paragraphs

Cause and effect paragraphs explain causes, or why something happens. They also explain effects, or what happens. Some events have more than one cause or effect.

Parts of Cause and Effect Paragraphs

- An introduction that tells the main cause or effect
- One or more causes
- One or more effects
- Transition words that help show the causes and effects
- Details from two or more texts that explain the causes and effects

Introduction
Tells the main effect

Causes
Tell the reason or reasons something happened

Effects
Tell other events that happen as a result

Details
Explain causes and effects

Every year, many birds migrate, or fly south for the winter. How do they know when it is time to go? Do they have calendars in their nests? No. Scientists have a few different ideas about **why** birds fly south.

According to *Birds*, some scientists think **cold weather makes birds** migrate south. In cold weather, there are not as many plants, fruits, or insects for birds to eat. **Because of this**, birds fly to where the weather is warmer and there is more food.

According to *The Bird Encyclopedia*, scientists think birds migrate **because** days grow shorter in the fall. When there is less sunlight, birds eat more food, which gives them extra energy. These scientists say that **this energy tells birds** to take off and begin their migration.

Other Transitions
So
Since
After that
The reason for

Name _____

Follow your teacher's directions to complete the frame.

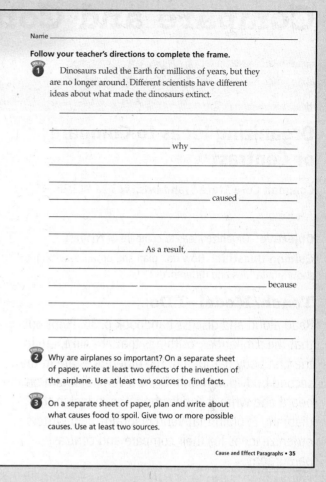

1 Dinosaurs ruled the Earth for millions of years, but they are no longer around. Different scientists have different ideas about what made the dinosaurs extinct.

_____

_____

_____ why _____

_____

_____

_____ caused _____

_____

_____ As a result, _____

_____

_____ . _____ because

_____

_____

2 Why are airplanes so important? On a separate sheet of paper, write at least two effects of the invention of the airplane. Use at least two sources to find facts.

3 On a separate sheet of paper, plan and write about what causes food to spoil. Give two or more possible causes. Use at least two sources.

✔ Corrective Feedback

IF . . . students are having difficulty thinking of different effects of an event,

THEN . . . have students list the people or things that could be affected by the event and then brainstorm possible effects. For example, if the cause is raising money for the school, students could list *students, teachers, the building,* and *the playground* as possibly being affected by the event. Guide students to brainstorm specific ways that raising money would affect the people and things on the list.

Focus Trait: Word Choice

Tell students that there are certain words writers use to point out cause and effect. Have students turn to the Other Transitions box on handbook p. 34. Have them help you brainstorm more words that signal cause and effect, such as *caused, causing, as a result, why, consequently, therefore.*

With students, practice writing sentences that use cause and effect signal words, such as, *I cleaned my room. As a result, I can find my books easily.* Have students add such signal words to their cause and effect paragraphs.

Compare and Contrast Paragraphs

Minilesson 23

Organizing Ideas to Compare or Contrast

Common Core State Standards: W.3.2a, W.3.2b

Objective: Organize ideas to compare or contrast.

Guiding Question: How do I plan and organize writing to show similarities and differences?

Teach/Model—I Do

Read aloud and discuss handbook p. 36. Point out that the similarities, or things that are alike, are in the first body paragraph. The differences are in the second body paragraph. Draw a Venn diagram on the board and write the ideas from the model in the diagram. Explain that Venn diagrams help writers organize ideas for their compare and contrast paragraphs.

Guided Practice—We Do

Have students name several familiar stories. Write titles on the board as students suggest them. Draw a Venn diagram. Select two of the titles and elicit similarities and differences between them. Guide students to think about characters, events, and settings. Together, complete the diagram. Write the differences in the two outer sections and the similarities in the overlapping middle section.

Practice/Apply—You Do

COLLABORATIVE Tell small groups to work together to complete a Venn diagram comparing two other titles. Have groups share their work.

INDEPENDENT Instruct students to pick two new titles and organize ideas about them in a Venn diagram.

Conference/Evaluate

Make sure students understand that the differences should make sense and be parallel. (*Apples and oranges have different colors* is a parallel; *Apples have leaves, but oranges are grown in Florida* is not.)

Minilesson 24

Drafting a Compare or Contrast Paragraph

Common Core State Standard: W.3.2

Objective: Write a compare and contrast paragraph.

Guiding Question: How do I show readers how things are alike and different?

Teach/Model—I Do

Have students review the definition, Parts of Compare and Contrast Paragraphs, and model on handbook p. 36. Discuss how compare and contrast words show similarities and differences. Go over the list of Other Words to Compare and Contrast. Remind students to add these linking words to help readers know what is being compared or contrasted.

Guided Practice—We Do

 Have students turn to the frame on handbook p. 37. Together, decide on two topics, such as *the sun and the moon*. Guide students to suggest similarities and differences. List their ideas in a Venn diagram. Use the diagram to help students create sentences that compare and contrast. Have students write in their books as you write on the board.

Practice/Apply—You Do

 COLLABORATIVE Have small groups work together to complete a Venn diagram and draft compare and contrast paragraphs for Activity 2.

 INDEPENDENT Have students read the directions for Activity 3. Tell them to use their prewriting plan from Lesson 12 or to brainstorm new ideas, using Graphic Organizer 14.

Conference/Evaluate

During the writing process, circulate and help students as needed. Evaluate using the rubric on p. 104.

- eBook
- WriteSmart
- Interactive Lessons

Compare and Contrast Paragraphs

Compare and contrast paragraphs tell how two things are alike and different. Details help explain the similarities and differences.

Parts of Compare and Contrast Paragraphs

- An introduction tells what will be compared and contrasted
- Details tell how the subjects are alike and different
- Linking words connect the ideas
- A conclusion sums up the paragraph

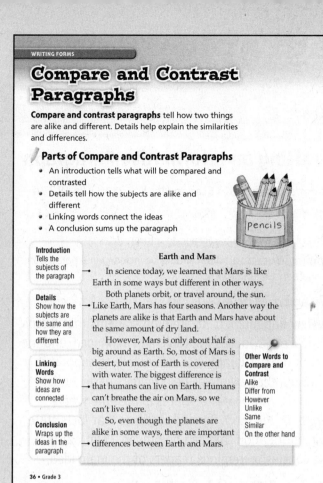

Introduction
Tells the subjects of the paragraph

Details
Show how the subjects are the same and how they are different

Linking Words
Show how ideas are connected

Conclusion
Wraps up the ideas in the paragraph

Earth and Mars

In science today, we learned that Mars is like Earth in some ways but different in other ways.

Both planets orbit, or travel around, the sun. Like Earth, Mars has four seasons. Another way the planets are alike is that Earth and Mars have about the same amount of dry land.

However, Mars is only about half as big around as Earth. So, most of Mars is desert, but most of Earth is covered with water. The biggest difference is that humans can live on Earth. Humans can't breathe the air on Mars, so we can't live there.

So, even though the planets are alike in some ways, there are important differences between Earth and Mars.

Other Words to Compare and Contrast
Alike
Differ from
However
Unlike
Same
Similar
On the other hand

Name _____

Follow your teacher's directions to complete the frame.

 Two subjects we have learned about this year are _____

_____ and _____

One thing these have in common is _____

_____

_____

_____ Another _____

_____

_____

However, _____

_____

_____

Unlike _____

_____

_____

So, _____

_____

 On a separate sheet of paper, write paragraphs that compare and contrast two story characters.

On a separate sheet of paper, use your prewriting plan to write compare and contrast paragraphs, or make a new plan to write about two activities you enjoy.

✓ Corrective Feedback

IF . . . students are having trouble discovering similarities and differences between their topics,

THEN . . . have them list attributes of each. Any characteristics that appear on both lists are similarities to compare; any characteristic that appears on only one list is a difference to contrast. For example, *apples grow on trees, are used to make juice, are great in pies, and are crunchy. Oranges grow on trees, are used to make juice, and are soft.* Similarities include: *grow on trees* and *are used to make juice.* Differences include: *apples are crunchy, but oranges are soft.*

Focus Trait: Word Choice

Remind students that compare and contrast signal words help show how ideas are related. Point out the words *both* and *another way* in the model on handbook p. 36. Explain that these show similarities between ideas, such as *Both planets orbit...the sun.* Point out the words *however* and *but* in the model and explain that these show differences, such as *However, Mars is only about half as big around as Earth.* Tell students that selecting an appropriate

compare and contrast word helps readers understand how the ideas are connected. Write:

> *One way John and Mary are _____ is that _____ are third grade students. _____ John is eight, _____ Mary is nine.*

Have students suggest compare and contrast words to fill in the blanks, such as *alike, both, on the other hand,* and *but.*

Informative Paragraph

Minilesson 25

Writing a Strong Topic Sentence

Common Core State Standard: W.3.2a

Objective: Write an effective topic sentence.

Guiding Question: How do I introduce the topic of an informative paragraph?

Teach/Model—I Do

Read aloud and discuss handbook p. 38. Point out that the first sentence is the topic sentence, which introduces the main idea of the paragraph. Explain that a strong topic sentence tells readers the subject of the paragraph and lets them know what will be proven or explained. The topic sentence in the model tells that the subject is the Appalachian Mountains and that the paragraph will explain that these are part of a huge, important mountain range. Explain that good writers use the topic sentence to clearly tell readers what information to expect in the paragraph.

Guided Practice—We Do

Help students name several topics studied in science or social studies such as *oceans* or *inventors*. Select a topic and guide students to write a strong topic sentence that states the subject and gives an idea of the information to come. (*Thomas Edison was an important scientist who invented many items we use every day.*) Write students' suggestions on the board.

Practice/Apply—You Do

COLLABORATIVE Have small groups select another topic from the board and write a topic sentence to introduce an informative paragraph about the subject. Have groups share their ideas.

INDEPENDENT Instruct students to select a different subject and write a topic sentence about it, or have them write a new topic sentence about the same subject.

Conference/Evaluate

Make sure students understand that a strong topic sentence not only names the subject but also introduces the main idea that will be discussed (ex: *I am writing about Mars* is not a strong topic sentence)

Minilesson 26

Drafting an Informative Paragraph

Common Core State Standards: W.3.2a, W.3.2b, W.3.2d

Objective: Write a paragraph to inform.

Guiding Question: What should be included in a paragraph to share factual information?

Teach/Model—I Do

Review handbook p. 38. Remind students that a topic sentence introduces the topic and main idea, and the rest of the paragraph includes details to support it. Point out that examples help readers easily understand the information (*That is almost the whole length of the U.S.*). Remind students that facts state true information that can be proven. Point out that the conclusion reminds readers of the main idea.

Guided Practice—We Do

 Have students turn to the frame on handbook p. 39. Discuss possible leaders to write about, and then select one together. Guide students to suggest reasons this leader was important. List suggestions on the board. Select three strong facts to support the main idea. Use student suggestions to complete the frame. Have students write in their books as you write on the board.

Practice/Apply—You Do

 COLLABORATIVE Have small groups work together to select a topic and complete Activity 2.

 INDEPENDENT Have students read the directions for Activity 3. Tell them to use their prewriting plan from Lesson 13 or to brainstorm new ideas using Graphic Organizer 7.

Conference/Evaluate

During the writing process, circulate and help students as needed. Evaluate using the rubric on p. 104.

- eBook
- WriteSmart
- Interactive Lessons

Informative Paragraph

An **informative paragraph** includes facts about a topic. It is written to teach or share true information.

Parts of an Informative Paragraph

- A topic sentence that introduces the main idea
- Facts and examples that support and explain the main idea
- True information that teaches about the topic

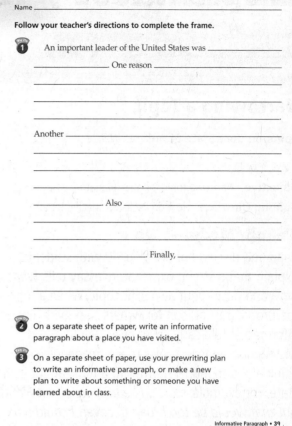

pencils

Topic Sentence
Introduces the main idea and tells what the paragraph is about

Supporting Details
Facts and examples explain the main idea

True Information
Teaches readers about the topic

Appalachian Mountains

The Appalachian (a-puh-LATCH-un) Mountains make up a huge, important mountain range. A *mountain range* is a row of mountains that are connected. The Appalachian Mountains are about 300 miles wide and 2,000 miles long. They run from Alabama to Canada. That is almost the whole length of the U.S. The mountains' highest point is in North Carolina. It is almost 7,000 feet tall, which is more than one mile high! One reason these mountains are important is that they divide the eastern and western parts of the U.S. They are also important because they were home to many Native American tribes. The mountains were named after the Apalachee Indians, who lived in what is now Florida. The Appalachian Mountains have been important to the United States for hundreds of years.

Other Transitions
First
Second
Next
Also
In addition
For example
Finally

Name _____

Follow your teacher's directions to complete the frame.

 1 An important leader of the United States was _____
_____ One reason _____
_____
_____

Another _____
_____
_____
_____ Also _____
_____
_____ Finally, _____
_____
_____

 2 On a separate sheet of paper, write an informative paragraph about a place you have visited.

3 On a separate sheet of paper, use your prewriting plan to write an informative paragraph, or make a new plan to write about something or someone you have learned about in class.

✓ Corrective Feedback

IF . . . students are having trouble selecting facts that strongly support the main idea,

THEN . . . review the difference between a fact and an opinion. Explain that the purpose of an informative paragraph is to teach information about the topic, so the writing should include information that can be proven, not the writer's thoughts about the topic. Guide students to locate facts about the topic in a reference book or online, if needed.

Focus Trait: Organization

Explain that in an informative paragraph, similar ideas are grouped together. Point out that in the model on handbook p. 38, information about the size of the mountains is in the beginning. This is followed by information explaining the highest point. Then, information about the reasons the mountains are important is at the end. Tell students that good writers organize their information in a way that will make sense to readers and help readers best understand the ideas. Write:

1. *Our moon rotates around Earth.*
2. *Humans reached the moon in 1969.*
3. *Mercury is the closest planet to the sun.*
4. *Jupiter is the largest planet.*
5. *Our planet has only one moon.*
6. *There are eight planets in our solar system.*

Have students form two groups with similar ideas (1, 2, 5 and 3, 4, 6).

Explanatory Essay: Prewriting

Minilesson 27

Narrowing a Topic

Common Core State Standard: W.3.2a

Objective: Narrow a topic for an explanatory essay.

Guiding Question: How do I select a specific topic?

Teach/Model—I Do

Read and discuss handbook p. 40 with students. Explain that a strong explanatory essay tells *what*, *why*, and *how* about a specific topic. When a topic is too broad, it is difficult for writers to provide enough information to clearly cover or explain it. Good writers narrow their topics to a manageable size. Think aloud to model narrowing a topic about your state. For example, say *I'd like to write about Florida, but that would be too broad to cover. I could tell about things visitors should see, but there are so many. I think I'll narrow my topic to a report about the Key West Aquarium.*

Guided Practice—We Do

Guide students to suggest several broad categories, such as sports, food, jobs. Together, select one category and write it at the top of an inverted triangle. Ask *How can we narrow this topic to make it more manageable for a report or essay?* Guide students to narrow the topic as you write in the triangle.

Practice/Apply—You Do

COLLABORATIVE Tell partners to select a different topic from the board and write it in an inverted triangle. Have them narrow the topic to make it specific enough to explain in one or two paragraphs.

INDEPENDENT Instruct students to choose a different topic and complete an inverted triangle to pinpoint a specific aspect of it.

Conference/Evaluate

Circulate and help students narrow their topics. Elicit more specific aspects of the topic for students to write about until they have a topic that is manageable.

Minilesson 28

Planning an Explanatory Essay

Common Core State Standards: W.3.2a, W.3.2b

Objective: Plan information that explains a topic.

Guiding Question: How do I plan my explanatory essay?

Teach/Model—I Do

With students, review handbook p. 40. Point out the topic sentence. Mention that details in an explanatory essay answer *what*, *how*, or *why* questions about the topic. Explain that the ideas in this model all answer *what* questions but that other topics may include answers to *how* or *why* questions.

Guided Practice—We Do

 Have students turn to the frame on handbook p. 41 and read the prompt aloud. Guide students to create a topic sentence. Have them suggest information to tell *what*, *how*, or *why* about the topic, such as *What does this job require? Why is it a good job?* List students' ideas on the board. Together select ideas to include in the organizer, and add supporting details. Have students write in their books as you write on the board.

Practice/Apply—You Do

 COLLABORATIVE Have small groups complete Activity 2. Tell them to include only the details that most strongly explain the topic.

 INDEPENDENT Have students read the directions for Activity 3. Tell them to use their prewriting plan from Lesson 14 or to brainstorm new ideas using Graphic Organizer 7.

Conference/Evaluate

During the writing process, circulate and help students select strong details. Evaluate using the rubric on p. 104.

Digital
- eBook
- WriteSmart
- Interactive Lessons

Explanatory Essay: Prewriting

An **explanatory essay** tells *what, why,* or *how* about a topic. It uses facts and details to explain the topic.

✏ Prewriting

- For an explanatory essay, begin by listing ideas for a topic. Think of things about which you would like to explain *what, how,* or *why.*
- Next, narrow the topic by selecting something specific about it to explore. Then, create an outline to organize facts.

Topic brainstorming

pets
cool jobs
police dogs

Narrowing the Topic

pets
learning about pets
how to get ready for
a new pet

Topic Sentence: There are important things to do to prepare for getting a new pet.

What, how, or why: Think about what kind of pet you can take care of.
Detail: some pets need a big yard, some pets need to be walked, your family might be allergic to some animals

What, how, or why: Find out what the new pet will need.
Detail: some pets need a cage, water bowl, running wheel, bed, collar, or leash

What, how, or why: Learn about what they need to eat.
Detail: some pets need pet food, some need vegetables

40 • Grade 3

Name _____

Follow your teacher's directions to complete this page.

1 Prompt: Think about a job you might like to have one day. Explain why this would be a great job for you.

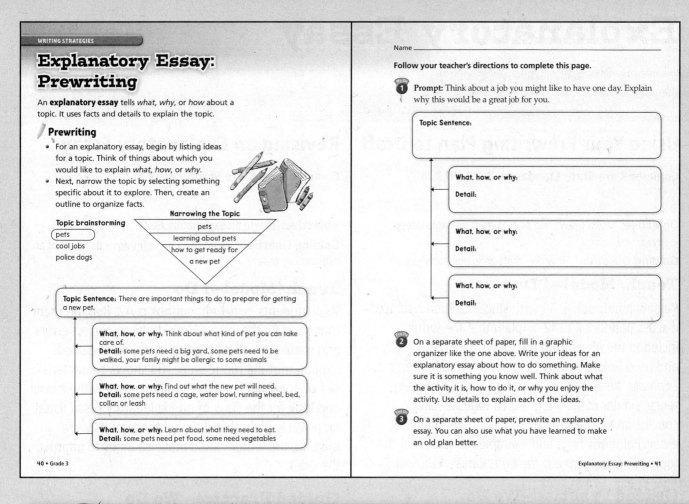

Topic Sentence:

What, how, or why:
Detail:

What, how, or why:
Detail:

What, how, or why:
Detail:

2 On a separate sheet of paper, fill in a graphic organizer like the one above. Write your ideas for an explanatory essay about how to do something. Make sure it is something you know well. Think about what the activity it is, how to do it, or why you enjoy the activity. Use details to explain each of the ideas.

3 On a separate sheet of paper, prewrite an explanatory essay. You can also use what you have learned to make an old plan better.

Explanatory Essay: Prewriting • 41

✔ Corrective Feedback

IF . . . students are having difficulty narrowing a topic sufficiently,

THEN . . . have them ask themselves, *Is there a certain idea about the topic that I could write about?* If the topic is still too broad, have them ask, *What is one smaller idea that I could explain about this topic?*

Focus Trait: Ideas

Explain that the first step to writing a strong explanatory essay is to select a good topic. Tell students that the topic should fit the writer's purpose. Ask students to identify the purpose of an explanatory essay (*to inform*). Explain that topics should be something writers can teach readers about.

On the board, write *Dogs.*

Explain that to write an explanatory essay about dogs, writers need to choose a specific topic about dogs that they can explain. Have students suggest ideas for possible topics such as *How to train police dogs, Breeds of dogs that are good with kids,* or *Teaching a dog to sit.*

Explanatory Essay

Minilesson 29

Using Your Prewriting Plan to Draft

Common Core State Standards: W.3.2a, W.3.2b

Objective: Use a prewriting plan to draft an explanatory essay.

Guiding Question: How do I draft an explanatory essay?

Teach/Model—I Do

Review handbook p. 40 with students. Then read and discuss handbook p. 42. Explain that the writer included the ideas from the prewriting in the draft and used linking words to connect the ideas *(first, for example, also)*. The essay begins with a topic sentence, similar ideas are grouped together, and a conclusion restates the main idea to wrap up the essay. Point out facts and examples that explain the topic. (*Pets need to eat the right kinds of things…*)

Guided Practice—We Do

 Have students open to the frame on handbook p. 41. Explain that students will use their prewriting to draft an explanatory essay. Have them turn to handbook p. 43. Point out the linking words in the frame. Guide students to use the prewriting as an outline, and have them suggest sentences to complete the frame. Elicit a conclusion for the essay. Have students write in their books as you write on the board.

Practice/Apply—You Do

 COLLABORATIVE Tell partners to use their prewriting from p. 41 to complete Activity 2, making sure to include linking words and a conclusion.

 INDEPENDENT Have students complete Activity 3 using their prewriting plan from Lesson 14 or plan and draft a new explanatory essay.

Conference/Evaluate

Remind students that their prewriting plan is an outline and that they can add details as needed while drafting.

Minilesson 30

Revising an Explanatory Essay

Common Core State Standard: W.3.5

Objective: Revise an explanatory essay.

Guiding Question: What can I do to improve the draft of an explanatory essay?

Teach/Model—I Do

With students, review handbook p. 42. Remind them that good writers revise their drafts to correct errors and make sure all parts of the form are included. Explain that the rubric on p. 104 shows characteristics of good writing. Have students review the model and look for the Parts of an Explanatory Essay listed on p. 42. Explain that if any of these parts were missing, the writer would make changes to improve the draft.

Guided Practice—We Do

Direct students to their drafts on handbook p. 43. Together, locate the parts of an explanatory essay. Ask questions such as, *What linking words are included? Are details grouped in a logical way? What details, if any, should be added to support the main idea? Are all verbs in the correct tense?* Make revisions on the board as students work in their books.

Practice/Apply—You Do

COLLABORATIVE Ask students to work in pairs to revise their draft from Activity 2. Remind them to refer to the rubric on p. 104 and Parts of an Explanatory Essay on handbook p. 42.

INDEPENDENT Have students revise their draft from Activity 3. Remind them to use the rubric.

Conference/Evaluate

During the writing process, circulate and help students improve their writing. Evaluate using the rubric on p. 104.

- eBook
- WriteSmart
- Interactive Lessons

Explanatory Essay

An **explanatory essay** explains *what*, *how*, or *why* about something. Facts, definitions, and details tell about the topic.

Parts of an Explanatory Essay

- A topic sentence that introduces the main idea
- Details, facts and definitions that explain the topic
- Information that is grouped together in a way that makes sense
- Linking words that connect ideas
- A conclusion that sums up the essay

Topic Sentence
Introduces the topic and tells the main idea

Linking Words
Connect details to the main idea

Details, Facts, and Definitions
Help to explain the topic and support the main idea

Conclusion
Sums up the essay

Preparing for a Pet

Are you thinking about adding a new animal friend to your family? If so, there are a few important things to do to prepare for getting a new pet.

First, think about what kind of pet you can take care of. For example, is your yard big enough to keep a pony? Is someone able to walk a dog while you are at school? Make sure you choose a pet that is best for your family.

Also, find out what your pet will need. For instance, a hamster will need a cage, a water bottle, and a running wheel. A puppy will need a collar and a leash. Finally, find out what kind of food your pet needs. Pets need to eat the right kinds of things to stay healthy

To be a good pet owner, you will need to be ready for your new friend.

Linking Words
And
Another reason
More
But
In addition

Name _____

Follow your teacher's directions to complete this page.

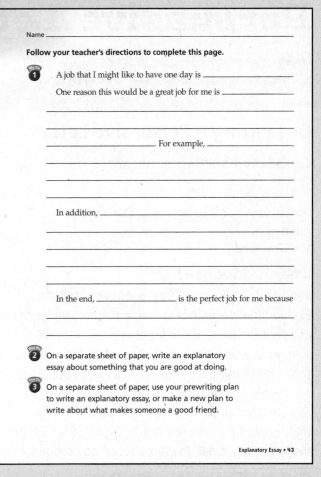

1 A job that I might like to have one day is _____

One reason this would be a great job for me is _____

_____

_____ For example, _____

_____

_____

In addition, _____

_____

_____

In the end, _____ is the perfect job for me because

_____

_____

2 On a separate sheet of paper, write an explanatory essay about something that you are good at doing.

3 On a separate sheet of paper, use your prewriting plan to write an explanatory essay, or make a new plan to write about what makes someone a good friend.

Corrective Feedback

IF . . . students are having difficulty transforming their prewriting into a draft,

THEN . . . remind them that the graphic organizer is simply a list of ideas. Explain that in the draft, these ideas should be explained and connected to form a cohesive piece of writing. Have them try using simple transitions such as *the first reason*, *the next reason*, and *the last reason* to link the ideas together. Remind them that a draft can be revised later to include more variety in linking words and that drafting is the stage when ideas are put into writing. Improvements and changes can be made later.

Focus Trait: Voice

Remind students that for an explanatory essay, a writer's voice should sound interested and knowledgeable about the topic. Explain that writers create this voice by using formal language.

On the board, write:

You should really find out a ton of stuff about cats before you get one.

Point out that this sentence uses informal language, which sounds like a conversation with a friend. Guide students to suggest ways to write the information using formal language. Example:

It is important to find as much information as possible about cats before getting one as a pet.

Persuasive Letter

Minilesson 31	**Minilesson 32**
## Organizing a Persuasive Letter	## Drafting a Persuasive Letter
Common Core State Standards: W.3.1a, W.3.1b	**Common Core State Standards:** W.3.1a, W.3.1b

Minilesson 31

Organizing a Persuasive Letter

Common Core State Standards: W.3.1a, W.3.1b

Objective: Use correct organization for a persuasive letter.

Guiding Question: How should I organize the parts of a persuasive letter?

Teach/Model—I Do

Read and discuss handbook p. 44 with students. Explain that the goal is stated in the first sentence and that the body of the letter includes reasons to support the goal. Explain that good writers organize their ideas before writing. Draw an idea-support map on the board. Write the goal from the model in the top box and supporting reasons beneath. Explain that the writer chose reasons to convince Mr. Harper, the school principal, to start a recycling program.

Guided Practice—We Do

Have students suggest topics and an audience for a persuasive letter. Together, select one topic, audience, and goal. Write students' ideas on the board. Elicit reasons to support the goal and use students' suggestions to fill in an idea-support map. Remind students that powerful, convincing reasons are most likely to persuade the reader to agree with the goal. Guide students to select the most convincing reasons to include in the organizer.

Practice/Apply—You Do

COLLABORATIVE Have small groups choose a goal for a persuasive letter to a teacher or principal. Instruct them to work together to complete an idea-support map with convincing reasons to persuade the reader.

INDEPENDENT Instruct students to complete an organizer for a persuasive letter to their parents. Have them include strong reasons to support their goal.

Conference/Evaluate

Circulate and help students select persuasive reasons. Ask, *What could you say to convince the reader that your goal is a great idea? What are the benefits of your idea?*

Minilesson 32

Drafting a Persuasive Letter

Common Core State Standards: W.3.1a, W.3.1b

Objective: Draft a persuasive letter.

Guiding Question: How do I write a letter to convince the reader to agree with my ideas?

Teach/Model—I Do

With students, review handbook p. 44. Point out the parts of a persuasive letter in the model; review letter form. Mention that the goal is clearly stated in the beginning. Point out examples of persuasive ideas in the model, such as *It would be very simple.* Explain that a positive, polite tone and strong reasons are effective ways to persuade an audience.

Guided Practice—We Do

 Have students turn to the letter frame on handbook p. 45. Explain that, together, you will use the organizer from Minilesson 31 to draft a persuasive letter. Elicit suggestions for a sentence that clearly introduces the goal. Guide students to suggest sentences for the body of the letter that include strong reasons and persuasive, polite words. Have students write in their books as you write on the board.

Practice/Apply—You Do

 COLLABORATIVE Ask students to work in groups to use their previous organizers to complete Activity 2. Remind them to include persuasive words and polite language.

 INDEPENDENT Have students read the directions for Activity 3. Tell them to use their prewriting plan from Lesson 16 or to brainstorm new ideas, using Graphic Organizer 7.

Conference/Evaluate

Circulate and help students select strong, convincing reasons to support their goal. Evaluate using the rubric on p. 104.

Digital
- eBook
- WriteSmart
- Interactive Lessons

Persuasive Letter

A **persuasive letter** is written to convince someone to agree with the writer's ideas. It explains the writer's views about a subject.

Parts of a Persuasive Letter

- A goal that is stated at the beginning
- Strong reasons that support the goal
- Correct letter form with a heading, inside address, greeting, body, closing, and signature
- A voice that is positive and polite

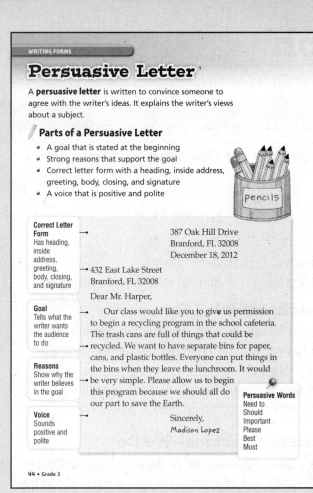

Correct Letter Form
Has heading, inside address, greeting, body, closing, and signature

387 Oak Hill Drive
Branford, FL 32008
December 18, 2012

432 East Lake Street
Branford, FL 32008

Dear Mr. Harper,

Goal
Tells what the writer wants the audience to do

    Our class would like you to give us permission to begin a recycling program in the school cafeteria.

Reasons
Show why the writer believes in the goal

The trash cans are full of things that could be recycled. We want to have separate bins for paper, cans, and plastic bottles. Everyone can put things in the bins when they leave the lunchroom. It would be very simple. Please allow us to begin this program because we should all do our part to save the Earth.

Voice
Sounds positive and polite

Sincerely,
Madison Lopez

Persuasive Words
Need to
Should
Important
Please
Best
Must

44 • Grade 3

Name _____

Follow your teacher's directions to complete the frame.

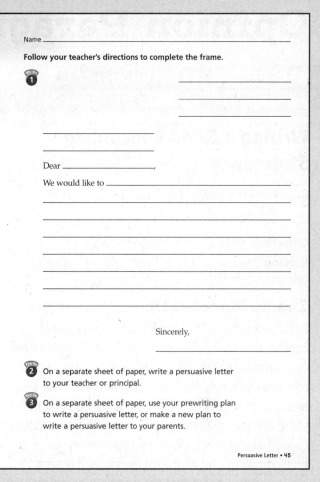

Dear _____,

We would like to _____

Sincerely,

_____

On a separate sheet of paper, write a persuasive letter to your teacher or principal.

On a separate sheet of paper, use your prewriting plan to write a persuasive letter, or make a new plan to write a persuasive letter to your parents.

Persuasive Letter • 45

✔ Corrective Feedback

IF . . . students are having difficulty stating supporting reasons in a convincing way,

THEN . . . have them think about why the goal should be important to readers or how it might benefit them. For example, if students want to convince their parents to let them stay up later on the weekend, they might write, *Allowing me to stay up late would give us more quality time to spend together.* Encourage them to state how the goal could positively affect the reader.

Focus Trait: Ideas

Explain that writers should express their ideas as specific statements so that the reader knows the purpose for the writing right away. Good writers state their ideas as a clear goal so that the reader understands exactly what the writer believes and what the writer wants the reader to do. Have students suppose they are writing a persuasive letter to you.

Write: *I do not like doing so much homework.*

Explain that this shows the writer's opinion but does not state the goal of the letter. In order to persuade someone, the topic must tell exactly what the writer wants, and the ideas must be detailed. Example:

I would like you to give us less homework on the weekends.

Opinion Paragraph

Minilesson 33

Writing a Good Concluding Statement

Common Core State Standard: W.3.1d

Objective: Write a concluding statement.

Guiding Question: How do I write a strong ending to an opinion paragraph?

Teach/Model—I Do

Read and discuss handbook p. 46 with students. Explain that the topic sentence introduces the writer's opinion and that the final sentence restates and reminds readers of the opinion. Read aloud the first and last sentences in the model. Point out that the same opinion is stated in both, using different words. Explain that a good concluding statement makes a final comment and wraps up the ideas. It leaves readers with a sense that the writing is complete.

Guided Practice—We Do

On the board, list several events the class has shared, such as *field trips, school assemblies, class activities*. Elicit students' opinions about two or three of the events, and guide them to write their opinions in a topic sentence *(Learning about people's jobs on Career Day was interesting)*. Then work together to restate each opinion in a concluding statement *(It was a lot of fun to learn about different types of careers)*. Record students' responses on the board.

Practice/Apply—You Do

COLLABORATIVE Have students work in pairs to write an opinion statement and a concluding statement about a movie or TV show they saw.

INDEPENDENT Instruct students to think of a food they like and write an opinion statement and a concluding statement about it.

Conference/Evaluate

Circulate and help students restate their opinions in a concluding statement. Remind them that restating means to state the same information in different words.

Minilesson 34

Drafting an Opinion Paragraph

Common Core State Standards: W.3.1a, W.3.1b

Objective: Draft an opinion paragraph.

Guiding Question: How do I write an opinion paragraph?

Teach/Model—I Do

Review handbook p. 46. Identify the opinion and supporting reasons. Point out details and examples that explain the reasons, such as *There was a real dinosaur skeleton*. Explain that the concluding statement repeats the opinion in a new way.

Guided Practice—We Do

 Have students turn to the frame on handbook p. 47. Ask students to share opinions about the topic. Write their responses on the board and select one to write about. Elicit reasons to support the opinion. Together, select the three strongest ones to include in the draft. Have students share interesting details and examples to support the reasons, as well as a concluding statement. Have students write in their books as you write on the board.

Practice/Apply—You Do

 COLLABORATIVE Have small groups complete Activity 2. Remind them to include interesting details and a conclusion.

 INDEPENDENT Have students read the directions for Activity 3. Tell them to use their prewriting plan from Lesson 17 or to brainstorm new ideas using Graphic Organizer 7.

Conference/Evaluate

During the writing process, circulate and help students select strong reasons to support their opinion. Evaluate using the rubric on p. 104.

 Digital • eBook • WriteSmart • Interactive Lessons

Opinion Paragraph

An **opinion paragraph** tells what the writer thinks about a topic. It also explains why the writer has this view.

Parts of an Opinion Paragraph

- A clear, interesting topic sentence that tells the writer's opinion
- Strong reasons that support the writer's opinion
- Interesting, convincing details that explain the reasons
- A closing sentence that repeats the opinion or makes a final comment

Topic Sentence
Introduces the writer's opinion

Reasons
Tell why the writer feels the way he or she does about the topic

Details
Explain the reasons

Closing Sentence
Repeats the opinion in a new way

A Day at the Museum

The science museum was the best field trip we took this year. One reason is because there were so many cool things to see there. For example, there was a real dinosaur skeleton. It was almost as tall as the roof. It was amazing to find out what it would feel like to stand beside one of these animals. We also got to do some neat activities. One thing we did was make fossils out of clay. I used a leaf. I pressed the leaf into the clay, and then I lifted it out. The leaf left a print in the clay, kind of like a fossil. Finally, we looked at bones from different animals. We used clues and pictures to figure out what animals they were from. The science museum was by far the most awesome trip we took all year!

Other Transitions
First
Second
Next
Another
Then
In addition

Name _____

Follow your teacher's directions to complete the frame.

 The best school assembly we had was _____
_____

The first reason _____
_____
_____
_____
_____
_____. Another reason _____
_____
_____
_____
_____. Also _____
_____
_____
_____
_____

 On a separate sheet of paper, write an opinion paragraph about an animal that you think would make a great pet.

On a separate sheet of paper, use your prewriting plan to write an opinion paragraph, or make a new plan to write about something you think would be interesting to study.

✔ Corrective Feedback

IF . . . students are having difficulty moving beyond their opinion,

THEN . . . have them look at each reason and ask themselves, *What can I do to convince someone to agree with my opinion?* For example, in the model, the student wrote, *We also got to do some neat activities.* The proof he offered was that they made fossils out of clay. This interesting example helped explain the activities. Encourage students to freewrite or talk to a partner to help them think of examples and proof to support each reason in the paragraph.

Focus Trait: Voice

Explain that good writers use a convincing voice when they write an opinion paragraph. That means they include powerful language to help convince readers to believe the opinion. Write: *It would be cool to learn about computers.* Explain that in order to persuade the reader, specific, powerful words should be used to create a convincing voice.

Write: *Dogs are good pets.*

Ask students to use specific, powerful words to help convince readers that this opinion is true. Examples:

Dogs are loyal companions and keep their owners from being lonely. Many types of dogs are protective of their owners. Many dogs are intelligent and obedient.

Problem and Solution Paragraph

Minilesson 35

Offering a Clear Solution to a Problem

Common Core State Standards: W.3.1a, W.3.1b

Objective: Write a clear solution to a problem.

Guiding Question: How do I clearly show one way to solve a problem?

Teach/Model—I Do

Read and discuss handbook p. 48 with students. Point out the problem and solution. Explain that the solution should clearly state one way to solve the problem and should be supported by reasons, facts, and examples to show why this would be effective. Point out how the writer of the model clearly identifies the solution (*One way to solve this problem…*) and includes supporting reasons. Read the reasons aloud.

Guided Practice—We Do

Have the class suggest problems faced by many students (*keeping their room clean, being on time*). Select one, and guide students to suggest clear solutions. Remind them that a clear solution shows readers exactly how to solve the problem. Write student suggestions on the board. Elicit supporting reasons for one of the solutions.

Practice/Apply—You Do

COLLABORATIVE Have students suggest problems they face when playing a game or doing an activity with friends. Write the suggestions on the board. Have partners choose one problem and write a clear solution, including supporting reasons, facts, or examples.

INDEPENDENT Have students choose a different problem from the board and write a clear solution with supporting details.

Conference/Evaluate

Remind students that a clear solution points out exactly how to solve the problem. Explain that readers should see exactly how the two are related.

Minilesson 36

Drafting a Problem and Solution Paragraph

Common Core State Standards: W.3.1a, W.3.1b

Objective: Write a problem and solution paragraph.

Guiding Question: How do I write a paragraph that discusses how to solve a problem?

Teach/Model—I Do

With students, review handbook p. 48. Point out that the beginning introduces the problem and then gives a clear solution. Explain that details and exact words such as *poison ivy*, *spruce trees*, and *sparks* clearly show why solving the problem is important.

Guided Practice—We Do

 Direct students to the frame on handbook p. 49. Have students suggest possible problems to write about. Together, select a problem and then ask students to suggest possible solutions. Help students choose one solution. Guide students to clearly state it; then elicit supporting reasons, facts, and examples to complete the frame. Have students write in their books as you write on the board.

Practice/Apply—You Do

 COLLABORATIVE Have pairs plan and complete Activity 2. Encourage them to use the clearly stated solution from Minilesson 35.

 INDEPENDENT Have students read the directions for Activity 3. Tell them to use their prewriting plan from Lesson 18 or to brainstorm new ideas using Graphic Organizer 7.

Conference/Evaluate

During the writing process, circulate and help students clearly state the problem and solution. Evaluate using the rubric on p. 104.

Digital
- eBook
- WriteSmart
- Interactive Lessons

Problem and Solution Paragraph

A **problem and solution paragraph** states a problem and a possible way to solve the problem.

Parts of a Problem and Solution Paragraph

- A problem that is clearly stated at the beginning
- A possible solution that is given
- Reasons, facts, and examples that support the solution and persuade readers to agree with it
- Exact words that explain the problem and solution

Problem
Introduced at the beginning

Possible Solution
Tells one way to solve the problem

Reasons, Facts, and Examples
Explain how the solution would be helpful

Tree Trouble

Our family enjoys camping in the woods, but we do not always know the names of the plants and trees we see there. This can be a major problem. Can you imagine walking through poison ivy because you do not know what it is? Itchy! One way to solve this problem is to take a nature guidebook with us. It shows pictures of different plants and tells about each one. A guidebook can teach us which plants are poisonous. Plus, we can read about which types of tree branches are best for making a campfire. For example, wood from spruce trees makes a lot of smoke. It can also throw sparks, which is not safe. A guidebook can teach us about the plants and help to keep us safe when we are camping.

Other Transitions
First
Second
Third
In addition
As well as
Another way
For instance

Name _____

Follow your teacher's directions to complete the frame.

1 Our family likes to _____, but one problem we face is _____

_____

We could solve this by _____

_____

_____

_____. The first reason _____

_____

_____

Another _____

_____

_____ For example, _____

_____

_____

_____

2 On a separate sheet of paper, write a problem and solution paragraph about a game or activity you do with friends.

3 On a separate sheet of paper, use your prewriting plan to write a problem and solution paragraph, or make a new plan to write about a chore you do at home.

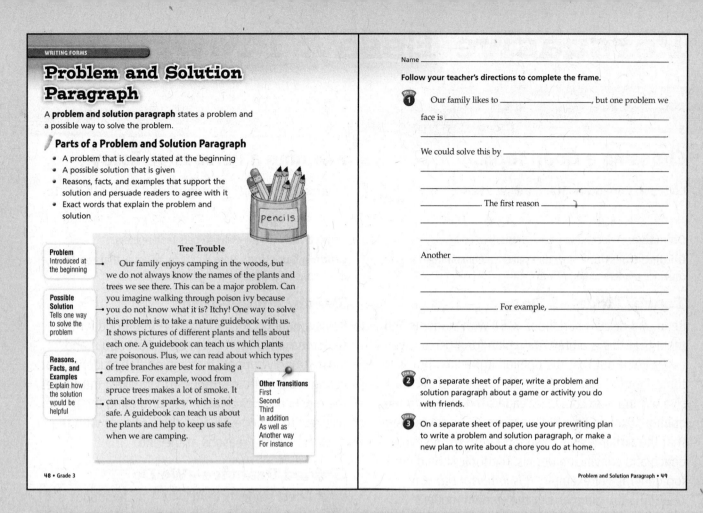

Corrective Feedback

IF . . . students are having trouble choosing solvable problems to write about,

THEN . . . suggest that they think of problems that affect their daily lives. Have students make a list of problems they face in specific areas of their lives, such as *home*, *school*, and *community*. Encourage them to use a graphic organizer, such as a web, to brainstorm problems and solutions.

Focus Trait: Word Choice

Tell students that good writers use exact words to help readers better understand their ideas. Precise words and phrases paint a clearer picture for readers than common, vague words. Write: *There is stuff all over my room.* Point out that this statement does not give readers a clear understanding of the problem. General words such as *stuff* do not give much information. Have students suggest exact words to improve the sentence. Example: *I can't find anything because there are stacks of library books and dirty laundry piled in every corner of my room.* Practice with another example, such as *No one wants to clean things up after a game.* Possible response: *No one wants to put the marbles and the board back in the box after playing Chinese checkers.*

Persuasive Essay: Prewriting

Minilesson 37	Minilesson 38

Choosing a Good Topic

Common Core State Standard: W.3.1a

Objective: Select a topic for a persuasive essay.

Guiding Question: How do I select an opinion that I want to convince readers to agree with?

Teach/Model—I Do

Read and discuss handbook p. 50 with students. Tell them that this is a prewriting plan for a persuasive essay. Point out that the opinion in the first box is the topic. Remind students that the purpose of persuasive writing is to convince readers to agree with the opinion. Explain that the topic should be something that the writer is able to support with strong evidence and convincing details. The topic should not be too general. For example, *It is important to stay healthy* is too general, but the student model's opinion statement is more specific.

Guided Practice—We Do

Ask students to suggest things that are important for kids to do, such as join a sports team, and write their suggestions on the board. Explain that you will select a topic for a persuasive essay and that the audience will be other students. Guide students to decide which topics are specific, supportable, and interesting to readers. Together, select one of the topics and write the topic as an opinion statement.

Practice/Apply—You Do

COLLABORATIVE Have small groups state opinions about important school subjects and then select which opinion would be the best topic for a persuasive essay.

INDEPENDENT Have students think about their favorite pastime and write a topic sentence to persuade readers that this is a valuable activity.

Conference/Evaluate

Encourage students to select a topic that can be supported with convincing evidence. Remind them that topics should be specific.

Planning a Persuasive Essay

Common Core State Standards: W.3.1a, W.3.1b, W.3.1d

Objective: Plan an essay to persuade readers.

Guiding Question: How do I plan an essay that convinces the audience to agree with my opinion?

Teach/Model—I Do

Review handbook p. 50. Explain that good writers select reasons that readers care most about and most strongly support the opinion. Tell students that listing reasons from strongest to weakest introduces the most convincing facts first; arranging them from weakest to strongest leaves the audience with the most convincing reasons at the end.

Guided Practice—We Do

 Direct students to Activity 1 on handbook p. 51. Use the topic from the We Do in Minilesson 37. Guide students to suggest supporting reasons for the opinion *Every kid should form a sports team.* Discuss which three reasons would be the strongest and how to most effectively arrange the ideas. Use student suggestions to fill in the organizer. Have students write in their books as you write on the board.

Practice/Apply—You Do

 COLLABORATIVE Have students work in groups to complete Activity 2, including only the strongest reasons in the organizer.

 INDEPENDENT Have students read the directions for Activity 3. Tell them to use their prewriting plan from Lesson 19 or to brainstorm new ideas using Graphic Organizer 7.

Conference/Evaluate

During the writing process, circulate and help students select strong reasons to support the opinion. Evaluate using the rubric on p. 104.

 Digital • eBook • WriteSmart • Interactive Lessons

Persuasive Essay: Prewriting

A **persuasive essay** gives reasons, facts, and examples to convince the reader to agree with a writer's opinion.

✏ Prewriting

- First, brainstorm possible topics. Think about topics that you have an opinion about and list them.
- Next, select a topic that you would like to convince readers to agree with. Use a graphic organizer to choose which ideas to include in your essay.

Topic brainstorming
Eating a healthy breakfast
Cleaning up our community
Getting enough exercise

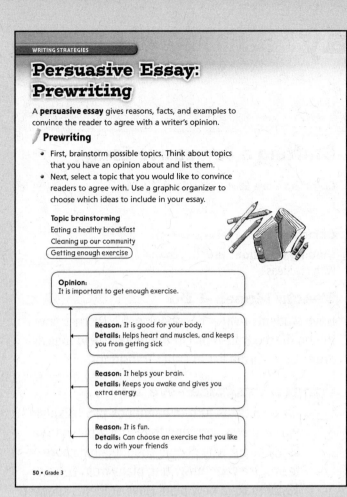

> **Opinion:**
> It is important to get enough exercise.
>
> > **Reason:** It is good for your body.
> > **Details:** Helps heart and muscles, and keeps you from getting sick
> >
> > **Reason:** It helps your brain.
> > **Details:** Keeps you awake and gives you extra energy
> >
> > **Reason:** It is fun.
> > **Details:** Can choose an exercise that you like to do with your friends

Name _____

Follow your teacher's directions to complete this page.

1 Topic: Something I think is important for kids to do

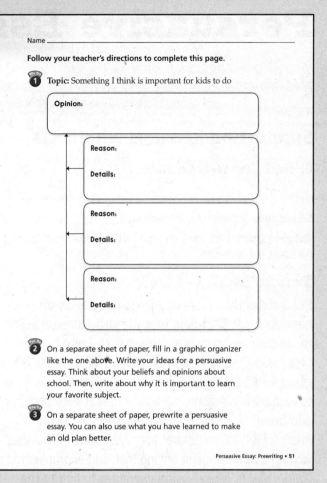

> **Opinion:**
>
> > **Reason:**
> >
> > **Details:**
> >
> > **Reason:**
> >
> > **Details:**
> >
> > **Reason:**
> >
> > **Details:**

2 On a separate sheet of paper, fill in a graphic organizer like the one above. Write your ideas for a persuasive essay. Think about your beliefs and opinions about school. Then, write about why it is important to learn your favorite subject.

3 On a separate sheet of paper, prewrite a persuasive essay. You can also use what you have learned to make an old plan better.

✔ Corrective Feedback

IF . . . students are having difficulty selecting which reasons to include,

THEN . . . have them select the reason they believe is the weakest and eliminate it from the list. Have students repeat this with the remaining reasons until only the strongest ones are left.

✏ Focus Trait: Ideas

Explain that when good writers plan a persuasive essay, they think about their audience. The purpose of the writing is to convince certain readers to agree with the opinion, so it is important to think about which reasons, examples, and details the readers would care most about. Write: *It is important to study for your spelling test each week.*

Have students suppose this is the topic of a persuasive essay and that the audience is the school principal. Ask what supporting reasons might be important to him (*Getting a good grade in spelling can help you get on the honor roll*). Then have them suppose the audience is other students and ask what supporting reasons might be important to them (*Being a good speller will help make your other homework much easier*).

Persuasive Essay

Minilesson 39

Supporting Reasons with Facts

Common Core State Standard: W.3.1

Objective: Support reasons with facts.

Guiding Question: How do I use facts and examples to persuade my audience?

Teach/Model—I Do

Read aloud the model of a persuasive essay on handbook p. 52. Explain that the writer used reasons to support an opinion about exercise. Point to the first reason the writer gives: *First of all, exercise is good for your body.* Explain that the writer uses facts to explain this reason, such as *it makes your muscles and bones healthy* and *it helps keep your heart healthy.* Tell students that they can make persuasive writing even more convincing by using examples to support facts. Model using examples to add to the fact about heart health, such as *Exercise can lower your blood pressure, which decreases your chance of heart disease.* Point out that examples are specific facts that give evidence to support an opinion.

Guided Practice—We Do

On the board, write a reason that people should learn to cook, such as *Cooking teaches you math skills.* Guide students to come up with one or two facts or examples to support the reason, such as *you have to make careful measurements.*

Practice/Apply—You Do

COLLABORATIVE Write another reason, such as *Homegrown food can be more healthful than store-bought food.* Instruct students to work together to list at least two facts to support the reason.

INDEPENDENT Instruct students to come up with another reason people should learn to cook. Then have them write two supporting facts or examples.

Conference/Evaluate

Have students make sure their facts and examples are true statements that can be proved. They should not use opinions to support their reasons.

Minilesson 40

Drafting a Persuasive Essay

Common Core State Standard: W.3.1

Objective: Write a persuasive essay.

Guiding Question: How do I convince someone to agree with my ideas?

Teach/Model—I Do

Have students review handbook p. 52. Discuss how the boldfaced transitions in the model show logical order. Go over the list of Other Transitions.

Guided Practice—We Do

 Have students turn to handbook p. 53. Explain that it shows a writing frame for a persuasive essay about why people should join a sports team. Use your prewriting plans from Lesson 19, or make a new plan. Have students suggest reasons to support the goal, such as *It teaches you about teamwork.* List reasons on the board. Use the list to elicit facts and examples to complete the frame in a logical order. Have students write in their books as you write on the board.

Practice/Apply—You Do

 COLLABORATIVE Have small groups work together to write a persuasive essay for Activity 2. Have groups share their writing.

 INDEPENDENT Have students read the directions. Tell them to use their prewriting plan from Lesson 19 or to brainstorm new ideas, using Graphic Organizer 7.

Conference/Evaluate

During the writing process, circulate and offer encouragement and help as needed. Evaluate using the rubric on p. 104.

WriteSmart CD-ROM

Persuasive Essay

- eBook
- WriteSmart
- Interactive Lessons

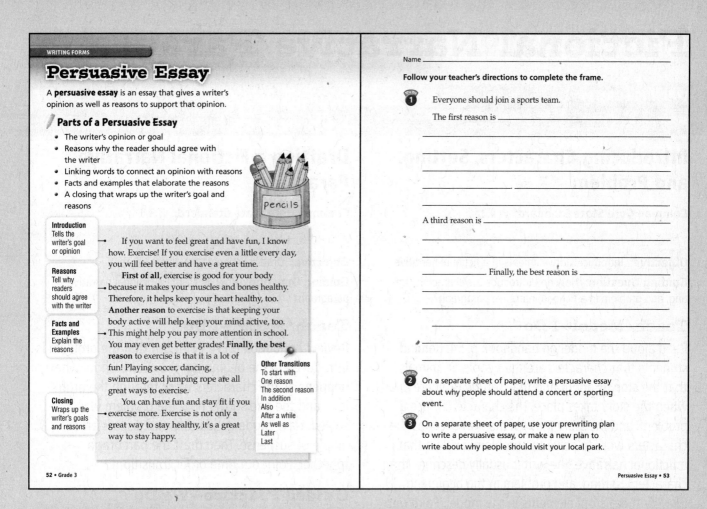

Persuasive Essay

A **persuasive essay** is an essay that gives a writer's opinion as well as reasons to support that opinion.

Parts of a Persuasive Essay

- The writer's opinion or goal
- Reasons why the reader should agree with the writer
- Linking words to connect an opinion with reasons
- Facts and examples that elaborate the reasons
- A closing that wraps up the writer's goal and reasons

Introduction
Tells the writer's goal or opinion →

Reasons
Tell why readers should agree with the writer →

Facts and Examples
Explain the reasons →

Closing
Wraps up the writer's goals and reasons →

If you want to feel great and have fun, I know how. Exercise! If you exercise even a little every day, you will feel better and have a great time.

First of all, exercise is good for your body because it makes your muscles and bones healthy. Therefore, it helps keep your heart healthy, too. **Another reason** to exercise is that keeping your body active will help keep your mind active, too. This might help you pay more attention in school. You may even get better grades! **Finally, the best reason** to exercise is that it is a lot of fun! Playing soccer, dancing, swimming, and jumping rope are all great ways to exercise.

You can have fun and stay fit if you exercise more. Exercise is not only a great way to stay healthy, it's a great way to stay happy.

Other Transitions
To start with
One reason
The second reason
In addition
Also
After a while
As well as
Later
Last

52 • Grade 3

Name _____

Follow your teacher's directions to complete the frame.

1 Everyone should join a sports team.

The first reason is _____

_____

_____

_____

A third reason is _____

_____

_____

_____ Finally, the best reason is _____

_____

_____

_____

2 On a separate sheet of paper, write a persuasive essay about why people should attend a concert or sporting event.

3 On a separate sheet of paper, use your prewriting plan to write a persuasive essay, or make a new plan to write about why people should visit your local park.

Persuasive Essay • 53

Corrective Feedback

IF . . . students are not giving enough support to their opinion,

THEN . . . have them brainstorm a list of facts about their topic that they can use to support their opinions. Explain that opinions are stronger when you can give readers examples that support them.

Focus Trait: Organization

Tell students that reasons within a body paragraph can be organized from weakest to strongest or vice versa. Direct students to the list of Other Transitions on handbook p. 52. Add more transitions, such as *the best reason*, *next*, and *most important*. Practice using these transitions to organize reasons by order of importance. For example, write, *To start with, milk has calcium that makes your bones strong.*

Second, milk doesn't contain as much sugar as soda and juice. Most important, milk tastes delicious! Discuss with students which order of reasons is the most convincing. Say, *I've decided to mention milk's delicious taste last because I think my audience cares more about taste, and I want them to remember this reason the most.* Have volunteers suggest other possible orders and explain why they would choose that organization.

Fictional Narrative Paragraph

Introducing Characters, Setting, and Problem

Common Core State Standard: W.3.3a

Objective: Introduce story elements in a fictional narrative.

Guiding Question: How do I introduce the characters, setting, and problem in a fictional narrative paragraph?

Teach/Model—I Do

Read aloud the model on handbook p. 54. Remind students that *characters* are the people or animals that the story is about and that *setting* is where and when the story takes place. The character(s) face a problem, and the story tells events that occur as the characters work to solve the problem. Explain that in a fictional narrative, the writer usually describes the characters, setting, and problem in the beginning. Identify these story elements in the model. Point out that the writer does not directly state where the story occurs, but details clearly reveal the setting.

Guided Practice—We Do

Help students suggest possible problems to include in the plot of a fictional narrative paragraph. Write their suggestions on the board. Select one problem together. Have students describe possible characters and settings for that problem. Use student ideas to write a two or three sentence descriptive introduction.

Practice/Apply—You Do

COLLABORATIVE Have small groups choose a different problem from the board and work together to write two or three sentences introducing the problem, characters, and setting.

INDEPENDENT Have students choose a different problem from the list and write to introduce the problem, characters, and setting.

Conference/Evaluate

Circulate and help students describe characters and setting. Explain that the description of a character is not only how he or she looks but also what he or she thinks or feels.

Drafting a Fictional Narrative Paragraph

Common Core State Standard: W.3.3

Objective: Draft a fictional narrative paragraph.

Guiding Question: How do I write a fictional narrative paragraph?

Teach/Model—I Do

Review handbook p. 54. Point out that the problem is introduced in the beginning, the events show what happens as the characters work through the problem, and the end shows how the problem was solved. Have students identify and discuss an example of suspense. Then draft the paragraph together. Point out time order transitions.

Guided Practice—We Do

 Have students turn to handbook p. 55. Explain that you will draft a fictional narrative paragraph about a character who has lost something. Guide students to suggest possible problems and then select one. Together, select and describe characters, setting, plot, and an element of suspense. Then draft the paragraph together. Have students write in their books as you write on the board.

Practice/Apply—You Do

 COLLABORATIVE Have small groups plan and complete Activity 2. Remind them to include transitions to show time order.

 INDEPENDENT Have students read the directions for Activity 3. Tell them to use their prewriting plan from Lesson 21 or to brainstorm ideas using Graphic Organizer 11.

Conference/Evaluate

During the writing process, circulate and help students use vivid descriptive words. Evaluate using the rubric on p. 104.

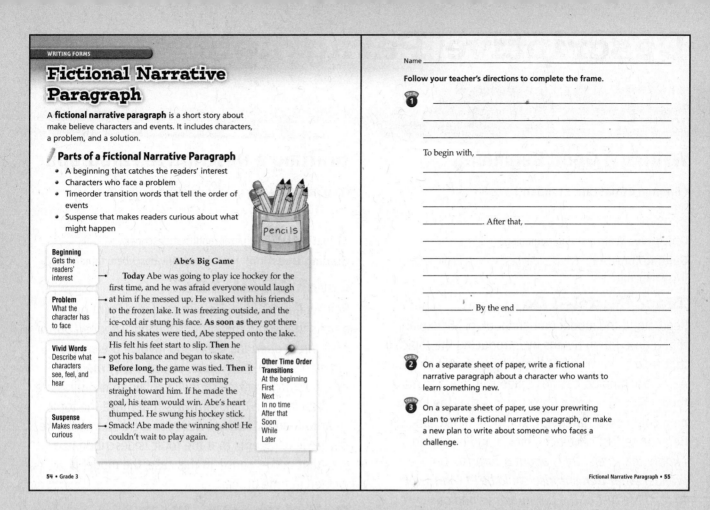

Fictional Narrative Paragraph

A **fictional narrative paragraph** is a short story about make believe characters and events. It includes characters, a problem, and a solution.

Parts of a Fictional Narrative Paragraph

- A beginning that catches the readers' interest
- Characters who face a problem
- Timeorder transition words that tell the order of events
- Suspense that makes readers curious about what might happen

Beginning Gets the readers' interest

Problem What the character has to face

Vivid Words Describe what characters see, feel, and hear

Suspense Makes readers curious

Abe's Big Game

Today Abe was going to play ice hockey for the first time, and he was afraid everyone would laugh at him if he messed up. He walked with his friends to the frozen lake. It was freezing outside, and the ice-cold air stung his face. **As soon as** they got there and his skates were tied, Abe stepped onto the lake. His felt his feet start to slip. **Then** he got his balance and began to skate. **Before long,** the game was tied. **Then** it happened. The puck was coming straight toward him. If he made the goal, his team would win. Abe's heart thumped. He swung his hockey stick. Smack! Abe made the winning shot! He couldn't wait to play again.

Other Time Order Transitions
At the beginning
First
Next
In no time
After that
Soon
While
Later

54 • Grade 3

Name _____

Follow your teacher's directions to complete the frame.

1 _____

To begin with, _____

_____ After that, _____

_____ By the end _____

2 On a separate sheet of paper, write a fictional narrative paragraph about a character who wants to learn something new.

3 On a separate sheet of paper, use your prewriting plan to write a fictional narrative paragraph, or make a new plan to write about someone who faces a challenge.

Fictional Narrative Paragraph • 55

Corrective Feedback

IF . . . students are having trouble including vivid details in their paragraphs,

THEN . . . have them imagine that they are standing beside the character. Ask, *What words describe what the scene looks like? What sounds do you hear? What three words best describe the character?* Have students include these ideas in their paragraph.

Focus Trait: Word Choice

Ask, *What is the setting of the fictional narrative paragraph on handbook p. 54?* Point out that the writer did not simply state *Abe was outside on a winter day.* Instead, he described the setting: *It was freezing outside; the ice-cold air stung his face; Abe stepped onto the lake.* Explain that good writers brainstorm ideas for descriptions that will clearly describe the setting.

Write: *He was at the beach.* Point out that this sentence tells the setting but does not paint a clear picture for the readers. Say: *He could feel the soft sand between his toes and the warmth of the sun on his face. The sound of the ocean waves crashing and the smell of the salty air made him smile.* Explain that these words set the scene by using vivid details to clearly describe the setting. Have students suggest ideas for describing other settings such as the circus or a ball game.

Descriptive Paragraph

Minilesson 43	**Minilesson 44**

Writing a Good Beginning

Common Core State Standard: W.3.3b

Objective: Write a strong beginning.

Guiding Question: What is the best way to begin a descriptive paragraph?

Teach/Model—I Do

Read aloud the model on handbook p. 56. Explain that a description begins by introducing the topic so that readers know what the paragraph will be about. A good beginning catches readers' interest to make them want to read on. Tell students that the beginning could be a statement, question, or exclamation. Reread the first sentence. Think aloud by saying, *I know that the story is about a surprise, but I wonder what that surprise could be! I can't wait to read the rest of the paragraph to find out.*

Guided Practice—We Do

Have students suggest several events, such as a school carnival or a class party, and list them on the board. Together, write a good beginning for a descriptive paragraph about the events. Guide them to introduce the topic in a way that makes the audience want to read on. Encourage them to suggest other ways to begin a description of the same topic using a question or exclamation.

Practice/Apply—You Do

COLLABORATIVE Have small groups select a different event and write two beginnings for a descriptive paragraph about the topic. Encourage students to use a variety of sentence types.

INDEPENDENT Have students choose a new topic from the board and write a sentence, question, or exclamation to begin a paragraph about the topic.

Conference/Evaluate

Encourage students to state the topic in an interesting way. *My birthday party was last week* may not encourage the audience to continue reading. *Do you know why my birthday party was the most amazing party ever?* will better catch readers' interest.

Drafting a Descriptive Paragraph

Common Core State Standards: W.3.3b, L.3.5a

Objective: Write a paragraph that describes.

Guiding Question: How do I clearly describe a topic?

Teach/Model—I Do

Review handbook p. 56 with students. Point out details that show the writer's feelings (*hopped out of bed, threw open the door*) and involve the senses (*smell of bacon, fluffy robe, sweet, sticky maple syrup, scratch-scratch sound*). Explain that similes are used to describe things in ways that make the topic clear to readers, such as *Her eyes were sparkling like glitter.* Tell students that the topic is described in a way that makes sense. In this case, the model is written in time order.

Guided Practice—We Do

 Have students to turn to the frame on handbook p. 57. Guide them to complete the topic sentence. Review the transitions in the frame and help students suggest events in order. Elicit sensory details, details that explain feelings, perhaps a simile to describe the topic. Have students write in their books as you write on the board.

Practice/Apply—You Do

 COLLABORATIVE Have pairs plan and complete Activity 2, including a simile and details involving at least two senses.

 INDEPENDENT Have students read the directions for Activity 3. Tell them to use their prewriting plan from Lesson 22 or to brainstorm new ideas using Graphic Organizer 15.

Conference/Evaluate

During the writing process, circulate and help students use similes to describe. Evaluate using the rubric on p. 104.

Digital
- eBook
- WriteSmart
- Interactive Lessons

Descriptive Paragraph

A **descriptive paragraph** explains what something is like. It creates a clear picture of the topic for the readers.

Parts of a Descriptive Paragraph

- A topic that is introduced at the beginning
- Words and details that show the writer's feelings
- Sensory details that tell how something looks, sounds, feels, tastes, or smells
- Similes that help explain what something is like
- Ideas that are organized in a clear order

Topic
Tells what the story is about

Similes
Describe what something is like

Sensory Details
Tell about the sights, sounds, smells, tastes, and feelings

Words and Details
Show the feelings of the writer

Speckles' Surprise

Yesterday I got the best surprise ever! The smell of bacon and pancakes woke me up early. My mom always makes my favorite breakfast on special days. I hopped out of bed and threw on my soft, fluffy robe. I skipped into the kitchen right away. While I chomped down the last bite of sweet, sticky, maple syrup-covered pancake, Mom said she had a special surprise for me. Her eyes were sparkling like glitter, so I knew it had to be something amazing. Just then I heard a scratch-scratch-scratch on the back door. Mom smiled and nodded. I was so excited that I threw the door open as fast as lightning, and it hit the wall with a loud BAM! My dog, Speckles, stood there, looking up at me with her round, dark eyes. Then I saw the tiny little balls of fur inside her dog house. Speckles had puppies!

Other Sensory Details
Glowing
Warm
Icy
Snap
Light
Squeaky
Feathery
Salty

Name _____

Follow your teacher's directions to complete the frame.

 The best day I ever had was _____

_____

I heard _____

_____

_____

_____ . The smell of _____

_____

_____

I saw _____

_____

_____

_____

_____

2 On a separate sheet of paper, write a descriptive paragraph about something that made you happy.

3 On a separate sheet of paper, use your prewriting plan to write a descriptive paragraph, or make a new plan to write about a great surprise.

✓ Corrective Feedback

IF . . . students are having difficulty using sensory details,

THEN . . . have them complete an idea web about the topic, such as Graphic Organizer 15, and include details or examples related to a different sense in each section. Ask guiding questions such as *What sounds were there? What did that feel like? Can you describe how that looked?* Then have students select sensory details from the web to include in their descriptive paragraphs.

Focus Trait: Word Choice

Explain that making a comparison is sometimes a good way to help readers understand a topic. For example, *Mr. Green is tall* does not tell readers how tall he is. *Mr. Green is tall as a palm tree* paints a clear picture. Explain that a simile is a comparison that uses the words *like* or *as*. Point out similes in the student model on handbook p. 56 (*Her eyes were sparkling like glitter; I threw the door open as fast as*

lightning). Explain that these similes describe what something is like in a way that is clear to the audience.

On the board, write, *The room was quiet.* Have students suggest similes to describe the room, such as *The room was as quiet as a sleeping baby; The room was as quiet as Sunday sunset.*

Dialogue

Minilesson 45	Minilesson 46

Writing Story Dialogue

Common Core State Standard: W.3.3b

Objective: Use dialogue to show how characters are different.

Guiding Question: How can I write dialogue that shows differences in my characters?

Teach/Model—I Do

Read aloud and discuss handbook p. 58. Point out the dialogue in the story. Ask what the characters' words show about them. Guide students to see that Laura is excited. Her mother is calm with a sense of humor. Retell the story, replacing dialogue with narrative, such as *Laura asked what was on her uncle's shoulder, and he told her it was his pet monkey.* Guide students to recognize that the dialogue makes the story more interesting. It shows the characters' feelings and personalities and helps move the story along. The dialogue also shows that the members of the family are playful and enjoy surprising one another.

Guided Practice—We Do

Have students name scary situations they could write about. Write suggestions on the board. Together, write sample sentences of dialogue that could show characters' feelings and personalities. Encourage students to show how characters are different. Continue until you have a list of at least three scary situations with samples of dialogue for each.

Practice/Apply—You Do

COLLABORATIVE Tell small groups to develop one topic from the list. Instruct students to work together to brainstorm additional dialogue to show differences between characters.

INDEPENDENT Have students develop a different topic from the list and write additional dialogue.

Conference/Evaluate

Have pairs conference to make sure the dialogue they have written sounds realistic. Each partner can read one person's part aloud and offer suggestions.

Punctuating Dialogue

Common Core State Standards: W.3.3b, L.3.2c

Objective: Use commas and quotation marks in dialogue.

Guiding Question: What punctuation should I use to show the exact words of my characters?

Teach/Model—I Do

Read aloud handbook p. 58. Guide students to recognize that quotation marks surround the characters' exact words but are not around the speaker's name. Ending punctuation is also enclosed in the quotation marks. Point out that a comma replaces the period at the end of a statement when the speaker's name follows his or her exact words; question marks and exclamation points are not replaced by commas.

Guided Practice—We Do

 Direct students to the frame on handbook p. 59. Together, decide on a topic and two or more characters to include in the story. Discuss personalities for each and what types of words they might use. Have students share ideas and write them on the board. Use their ideas to complete the frame together, having students tell how to punctuate dialogue. Have students write in their books as you write on the board.

Practice/Apply—You Do

 COLLABORATIVE Have small groups complete Activity 2, using a variety of sentence types and correct punctuation.

 INDEPENDENT Have students use their prewriting plan from Lesson 23 or brainstorm new ideas using Graphic Organizer 10.

Conference/Evaluate

During the writing process, circulate and help students as needed. Evaluate using the rubric on p. 104.

Digital
- eBook
- WriteSmart
- Interactive Lessons

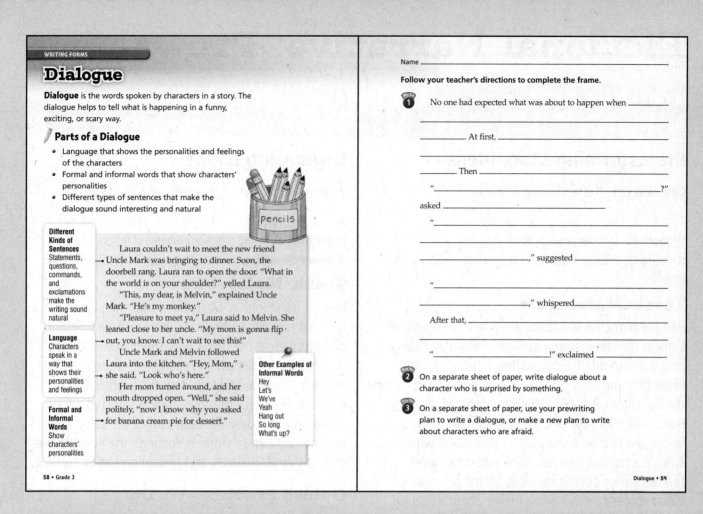

Dialogue

Dialogue is the words spoken by characters in a story. The dialogue helps to tell what is happening in a funny, exciting, or scary way.

Parts of a Dialogue

- Language that shows the personalities and feelings of the characters
- Formal and informal words that show characters' personalities
- Different types of sentences that make the dialogue sound interesting and natural

Different Kinds of Sentences
Statements, questions, commands, and exclamations make the writing sound natural

Language
Characters speak in a way that shows their personalities and feelings

Formal and Informal Words
Show characters' personalities

Laura couldn't wait to meet the new friend Uncle Mark was bringing to dinner. Soon, the doorbell rang. Laura ran to open the door. "What in the world is on your shoulder?" yelled Laura.

"This, my dear, is Melvin," explained Uncle Mark. "He's my monkey."

"Pleasure to meet ya," Laura said to Melvin. She leaned close to her uncle. "My mom is gonna flip out, you know. I can't wait to see this!"

Uncle Mark and Melvin followed Laura into the kitchen. "Hey, Mom," she said. "Look who's here."

Her mom turned around, and her mouth dropped open. "Well," she said politely, "now I know why you asked for banana cream pie for dessert."

Other Examples of Informal Words
Hey
Let's
We've
Yeah
Hang out
So long
What's up?

Name _____

Follow your teacher's directions to complete the frame.

1 No one had expected what was about to happen when _____

_____ At first, _____

_____ Then _____

"_____?"

asked _____

"_____

_____," suggested _____

"_____

_____," whispered _____

After that, _____

"_____!" exclaimed _____

2 On a separate sheet of paper, write dialogue about a character who is surprised by something.

3 On a separate sheet of paper, use your prewriting plan to write a dialogue, or make a new plan to write about characters who are afraid.

Corrective Feedback

IF . . . students are having trouble using dialogue to show differences between characters,

THEN . . . have them use Graphic Organizer 15 to brainstorm ideas about the characters' personalities. Students can use this information to decide how the characters would react to situations in the story and what types of words each would use. For example, if a web about a character includes words like *shy, smart, quiet,* then the character might likely use dialogue such as "I...I think I might know how to solve the mystery," whispered Jenny.

Focus Trait: Voice

Remind students that the words a writer chooses show his or her voice. Explain that dialogue shows the voices of the characters. The words of the characters should sound like what they might actually say. Informal words, slang, and contractions are often used by children, in conversation between friends, and in casual situations. More formal language and longer words are often used by adults or professionals. Short sentences and exclamations show excitement, whereas questions can show uncertainty or nervousness. Write: *We are anxious to attend the upcoming event.* Have students suggest what type of character might speak these words, then suggest how the dialogue might sound if spoken by a child: Example: *We're going to the party on Saturday! I can't wait!*

Fiction 1 Narrative: Prewriting

Minilesson 47

Brainstorming Story Ideas

Common Core State Standard: W.3.3a

Objective: Consider possible fictional plots.

Guiding Question: How do I come up with ideas to write about?

Teach/Model—I Do

Read and discuss handbook p. 60 with students. Explain that *brainstorming* means listing any ideas that come to mind. Good writers brainstorm story ideas first and then consider which idea would make the best story. Point out the list of topic ideas on the handbook page. Explain that the student writer was instructed to plan a story about characters who survive a natural disaster. Think aloud to model brainstorming additional ideas for the prompt: *What comes to mind when I think about a natural disaster? It could be a tornado, a volcano erupting, or a wildfire. I could write a story about one of these.*

Guided Practice—We Do

Guide students to brainstorm a list of dangerous or scary situations. Remind them to brainstorm as many ideas as possible. Encourage students to suggest ideas as they come to mind. Write their ideas on the board. Continue until the list includes 7 or 8 ideas.

Practice/Apply—You Do

COLLABORATIVE Have small groups work together to brainstorm a list of big events that must be planned for in advance, such as a party. Encourage students to include at least 4 or 5 ideas and then share their lists.

INDEPENDENT Have students brainstorm types of competitions, such as football games or a spelling bee. Encourage students to list at least 4 or 5 ideas.

Conference/Evaluate

Remind students that they do not need to select a single topic to write about at this point. Encourage creative thinking and remind students that there are no right or wrong ideas.

Minilesson 48

Organizing a Plot

Common Core State Standards: W.3.3a, W.3.3d

Objective: Plan and organize elements of fiction.

Guiding Question: How do I organize the events of a plot?

Teach/Model—I Do

Review handbook p. 60. Explain that the plot of a fictional narrative introduces the characters, setting, and problem at the beginning. The middle includes events that show how the characters try to solve the problem, and the end tells how the problem is resolved. Point out that the student selected a topic and organized ideas for each part of the story. Point out the problem (a storm is coming), the event in the middle (family waited), and resolution (storm turned).

Guided Practice—We Do

 Direct students to turn to Activity 1 on handbook p. 61. Together, select a topic from the brainstorm list in Minilesson 47. Have students suggest a setting and characters as well as a problem, events, and resolution. Together, select the best ideas and use them to complete the organizer. Have students write in their books as you write on the board.

Practice/Apply—You Do

 COLLABORATIVE Have small groups plan and complete Activity 2. Encourage them to select a topic from their brainstorm list.

 INDEPENDENT Have students read directions for Activity 3. Tell them to use their prewriting plan from Lesson 24 or to brainstorm new ideas using Graphic Organizer 10.

Conference/Evaluate

During the writing process, circulate and help students think of events leading to the resolution. Evaluate using the rubric on p. 104.

- eBook
- WriteSmart
- Interactive Lessons

Fictional Narrative: Prewriting

A fictional narrative is a made-up story that tells about characters who solve a problem. It has a plot told in time order.

Prewriting

- First, brainstorm a list of possible plots.
- Next, choose a plot to write about. Use a graphic organizer to list ideas for setting, characters, and events.

Topic brainstorming

Staying safe in a storm
A family's first earthquake
What happened when a town flooded

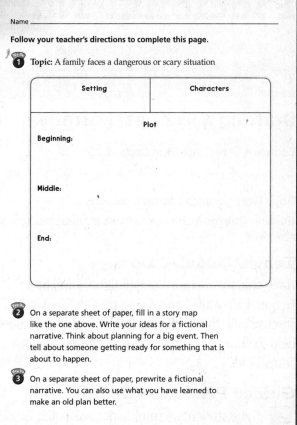

Setting	Characters
Home	Jada, Jada's Mom
Plot	

Beginning:
An emergency signal is on the radio telling them that a bad rainstorm is coming.

Middle:
The family waits in the kitchen where they will be safe.

End:
The radio tells that the storm has turned and the weather is safe.

Name _____

Follow your teacher's directions to complete this page.

1 **Topic:** A family faces a dangerous or scary situation

Setting	Characters
Plot	

Beginning:

Middle:

End:

2 On a separate sheet of paper, fill in a story map like the one above. Write your ideas for a fictional narrative. Think about planning for a big event. Then tell about someone getting ready for something that is about to happen.

3 On a separate sheet of paper, prewrite a fictional narrative. You can also use what you have learned to make an old plan better.

✔ Corrective Feedback

IF . . . students are having difficulty determining where to list the events for their fictional narrative,

THEN . . . have them freewrite everything they imagine happening to their characters. Encourage them to list events in whatever order they come to mind. Then, have partners work together to arrange events in time order using Graphic Organizer 10 as a guide. Partners should help each other to remove unrelated events and add missing events.

Focus Trait: Ideas

Tell students that in a fictional narrative, the problem is introduced in the beginning and solved at the end. Students can think of ideas for story endings by freewriting responses to the following questions:

How do my characters feel after solving the problem? What do my characters say? How do my characters act?

Have students use the best ideas from their responses as endings.

Fictional Narrative

Minilesson 49	Minilesson 50

Drafting a Fictional Narrative

Common Core State Standard: W.3.3

Objective: Compose a fictional narrative.

Guiding Question: How do I express my ideas in a fictional narrative?

Teach/Model—I Do

Have students review the definition, Parts of a Fictional Narrative, and model on handbook p. 62. Discuss how the boldfaced transitions in the model help to show time order. Go over the list of Other Transitions.

Guided Practice—We Do

 Have students turn to handbook p. 63. Guide them to use their prewriting plans from Lesson 24 to complete the frame. Help students suggest story details and dialogue. List their ideas. Together, use the list to create sentences to complete the frame. Encourage students to begin the frame by introducing characters and setting. Have students write in their books as you write on the board.

Practice/Apply—You Do

 COLLABORATIVE Have partners work together to write a story for Activity 2 in which they choose and write about another topic. Have them share their writing.

 INDEPENDENT Have students read the directions. Tell them to use their prewriting plan from Lesson 24 or to brainstorm new ideas using Graphic Organizer 10.

Conference/Evaluate

During the writing process, circulate and offer encouragement and help. Point out opportunities to use dialogue to reveal characters' personalities. Evaluate using the rubric on p. 104.

WriteSmart CD-ROM
Fictional Narrative [Story (w/ dialogue)]

Revising a Fictional Narrative

Common Core State Standards: W.3.3, W.3.4

Objective: Revise a fictional narrative.

Guiding Question: How can I improve my fictional narrative draft?

Teach/Model—I Do

Review handbook p. 62. Remind students that a strong fictional narrative has all of the elements listed in the Parts of a Fictional Narrative list. Tell students that one important revision they can make is to improve their dialogue. Point out how dialogue shows each character's feelings. Mom's dialogue illustrates her calmness, such as when she says, *"We have to get in the closet."* Jada's dialogue shows her panic, such as when she cries, *"Oh no! What should we do?"* Remind students that dialogue should show characters' personalities while making the story interesting.

Guided Practice—We Do

Have students turn to their drafts on handbook p. 63. Together, revise the frame, adding dialogue that shows characters' personalities. Guide students to brainstorm additional dialogue to show differences between characters in the draft.

Practice/Apply—You Do

COLLABORATIVE Have partners revise their drafts from Activity 2 on handbook p. 63. Encourage students to use dialogue to show how characters are different.

INDEPENDENT Instruct students to revise their fictional narrative drafts from Activity 3, adding dialogue that shows readers about the characters.

Conference/Evaluate

Have pairs conference to make sure the dialogue they have written sounds realistic. Each partner can read one person's part aloud and offer suggestions.

Digital ▸ • eBook • WriteSmart • Interactive Lessons

Fictional Narrative

A **fictional narrative** tells about characters who face a problem. The plot is usually told in time order, or sequence, and shows how the characters solve the problem.

Parts of a Fictional Narrative

- A plot with a beginning, a middle, and an end
- Characters, a setting, and a problem that are introduced in the beginning
- Dialogue that shows characters' feelings
- Vivid details to create a clear picture for readers
- An end that shows how the problem is solved

Beginning
Introduces the characters, setting, and problem

Middle
Vivid details show how the characters work to solve the problem

Dialogue
Shows characters' feelings

End
Shows how the problem is solved

A loud, terrible noise from the TV filled Jada's room. "What is that screaming?" she asked.

"It's an emergency signal," Mom explained. **Just then**, a man's deep voice came on. He said there was a tornado warning.

"Oh no! What should we do?" Jada cried.

"We have to get in the closet," her mom said. She grabbed the radio from the kitchen counter. They dashed to Mom's bedroom closet. They huddled together on the floor.

"If there's a tornado, it is best to be away from doors and windows. We need to be in the middle of the house, not by the outside walls," Mom said. **While** they waited, they listened to the radio. **Soon**, the tornado passed.

"I am glad that's over," said Jada. "I would rather curl up on the couch than in the closet!"

Other Transitions
First
Next
After that
As
During
After a while
Meanwhile
Later
Finally

Name _____

Follow your teacher's directions to complete the frame.

1 _____
_____
_____ Just then, _____
_____
_____ While _____
_____ Soon, _____
_____
_____
_____
_____
_____
_____
_____ Following that, _____
_____
_____ Last, _____
_____

2 On a separate sheet of paper, write a fictional narrative about some unusual weather.

3 On a separate sheet of paper, use your prewriting plan to write a story, or make a new plan for a story about a natural disaster or other unusual situation.

✔ Corrective Feedback

IF . . . students have not sufficiently developed the middle of their story,

THEN . . . remind them that the middle of the story shows the action and tells the events that lead up to the problem being solved. Explain that the characters' words and actions help build suspense and keep readers interested. Remind them to use dialogue and vivid details that paint a picture for the readers. They should also show what begins to happen to solve the problem.

Focus Trait: Word Choice

Tell students that metaphors and similes can help paint a clear picture for the reader. On the board, write:

There was snow on the ground.

Ask *How much snow was on the ground? What did it look like?* Then write:

Blankets of snow covered the ground.

Point out the vivid words: *blankets* and *covered the ground.* Explain that this metaphor creates a clear

picture of what the snow looked like. Point out that sentences beginning with the words *There was* or *It was* can often be revised to be stronger. Then write:

It was dark during the storm.

Have students suggest vivid words, and write revised sentences on the board.

Example: *The sky was as black as ink during the storm.*

Compare and Contrast Paragraph

Minilesson 51

Organizing Ideas to Compare and Contrast

Common Core State Standards: W.3.2a, W.3.2b

Objective: Organize ideas to compare and contrast.

Guiding Question: How do I plan and organize writing to show similarities and differences?

Teach/Model—I Do

Read aloud and discuss handbook p. 64. Point out some of the similarities and differences the author writes about in the model. Draw a Venn diagram on the board, and write the ideas from the model in the diagram. Explain that Venn diagrams help organize ideas to compare and contrast before writing.

Guided Practice—We Do

Have students name several familiar stories. Write titles on the board as students suggest them. Draw a Venn diagram. Select two of the titles and guide students to think about characters, events, and settings. Then have students discuss similarities and differences between the two stories. Together, complete the diagram. Write the differences in the two outer sections and write the similarities in the overlapping middle section.

Practice/Apply—You Do

COLLABORATIVE Tell partners to work together to complete a Venn diagram comparing and contrasting two of the other titles. Have them share their work.

INDEPENDENT Instruct students to pick two new titles and organize ideas about them in a Venn diagram.

Conference/Evaluate

Make sure students understand that the differences they include should make sense and be parallel. For example, *Birds have two legs but dogs have four* is a parallel difference. *Apples have leaves, but oranges grow in Florida* is not a parallel example.

Minilesson 52

Drafting a Compare and Contrast Paragraph

Common Core State Standard: W.3.2

Objective: Write a compare and contrast paragraph.

Guiding Question: How do I show readers how things are alike and different?

Teach/Model—I Do

Have students review the definition, Parts of a Compare and Contrast Paragraph, and the model on handbook p. 64. Point out a comparing or contrasting sentence, such as *...they are both about animals that talk.*

Guided Practice—We Do

 Have students turn to Frame 1 on handbook p. 65. Together, decide on two familiar texts to compare. Guide students to use their Venn diagrams from the We Do in Minilesson 51 to complete the frame. Have students write in their books as you write on the board.

Practice/Apply—You Do

 COLLABORATIVE To complete Frame 2, have partners work together to contrast the same two texts they just used in the We Do. Have partners share their writing.

 INDEPENDENT Have students read the directions. Tell them to use their prewriting plan from Lesson 26 or to brainstorm new ideas, using Graphic Organizer 14.

Conference/Evaluate

During the writing process, circulate and offer encouragement and help as needed. Evaluate using the rubric on p. 104.

WriteSmart CD-ROM

Compare and Contrast Paragraph / Essay

 Digital
• eBook
• WriteSmart
• Interactive Lessons

Compare and Contrast Paragraph

When you **compare and contrast** two texts, you explain how the texts are alike and how they are different.

Parts of a Compare and Contrast Paragraph

- A topic sentence that names the texts
- A stated main idea for each paragraph
- Sentences that tell how the texts are alike
- Sentences that tell how they are different
- A closing that sums up your ideas

Topic Sentence
Names the texts

Comparing Sentences
Tell how the texts are the same

Contrasting Sentences
Tell how the texts are different

Closing
Sums up what is important

→ *Charlotte's Web* and *The Trumpet of the Swan* are alike in some ways. They are alike because E. B. White wrote both books, and they are both about animals that talk. Another thing that is alike in both books is how smart the animals are. In each book a kid makes friends with the animals, too. The two books are different, too. *Charlotte's Web* is about a pig and a spider, and it happens on a farm. *Trumpet of the Swan* is about birds, and it happens in the wild. Also, the books are illustrated by different people. Still, I think they are more alike than different.

Other Transitions
In addition
Similar
As well
On the other hand
Neither

Name _____

Follow your teacher's directions to complete Frames 1 and 2.

 In some ways, _____ and

_____ are alike. They both _____

_____

They also _____

_____

_____

_____

_____

 Some things about the books are different, too. _____

_____

_____

_____

_____

_____

I think _____

3 On a separate sheet of paper, write a compare and contrast paragraph about two books you have read.

✔ Corrective Feedback

IF . . . students are having trouble organizing ideas to compare and contrast,

THEN . . . have them use different color crayons to identify their ideas. They can use a red crayon to underline the ideas in the left circle of their Venn diagram, a blue crayon to underline the ideas in the right circle, and a purple crayon to underline ideas in the overlapping section. Guide them to use the purple ideas in a paragraph that compares and the red and blue ideas in a paragraph that contrasts.

Focus Trait: Organization

Remind students that the topic sentence of a compare and contrast paragraph introduces the two things being compared and contrasted. The topic sentence also clearly states whether the paragraph will compare or contrast.

On the board, write *textbook* and *newspaper*. Tell students you want to write a topic sentence for a paragraph that compares these two things. Write:

Textbooks and newspapers are similar in several ways.

Underline the word *similar*, and explain that it tells readers that the paragraph will compare.

Then elicit suggestions for a topic sentence that clearly introduces a contrast paragraph, such as:

You may have noticed many ways that textbooks are different from newspapers.

Problem/Solution Paragraph

Minilesson 53

Writing a Strong Beginning

Common Core State Standard: W.3.2a

Objective: Write a strong beginning.

Guiding Question: How do I word the beginning of a paragraph in a way that catches the readers' attention?

Teach/Model—I Do

Read and discuss handbook p. 66 with students. Point out that the first sentence is a question that draws readers into the paragraph. Explain that beginning with a question, a quote, an interesting fact, or an anecdote are great ways to catch readers' interest. Suggest other beginnings to the paragraph such as *One of the light bulbs at Thomas Edison's home was never turned off from the time he invented it. But this is not a good habit for us to practice.*

Guided Practice—We Do

On the board, help students list several problems that they face, such as keeping up with chores or selecting an activity to do with friends. Guide students to suggest strong beginnings for a problem/solution paragraph about one of the topics. Encourage students to include a question, quote, fact, or anecdote. Write students' suggestions on the board.

Practice/Apply—You Do

COLLABORATIVE Have small groups select a problem from the board and write two strong beginnings. Encourage them to use different formats for each, such as one question and one quote.

INDEPENDENT Instruct students to choose a different topic and write two possible beginnings for a problem/solution paragraph.

Conference/Evaluate

Circulate and guide students to reword statements as questions or to think of an interesting anecdote.

Minilesson 54

Drafting a Problem/Solution Paragraph

Common Core State Standards: W.3.2b, W.3.2d

Objective: Draft a problem/solution paragraph.

Guiding Question: How do I explain one way to solve a problem?

Teach/Model—I Do

Review handbook p. 66. Identify the problem, solution, and details. Point out that examples are grouped with similar ideas and that a conclusion reminds readers why the solution is effective. Explain that clear details help to explain the writer's ideas.

Guided Practice—We Do

 Have students turn to the frame on handbook p. 67. Together, select a problem and a solution to complete the frame. Have students suggest reasons the solution would be helpful, and facts and examples to support the reasons. Guide students to organize the details in a logical sequence and to suggest a conclusion for the paragraph. Have students write in their books as you write on the board.

Practice/Apply—You Do

 COLLABORATIVE Have students work in groups to complete Activity 2. Remind them to include reasons, facts, and details to explain why the solution would be helpful.

 INDEPENDENT Have students read the directions for Activity 3. Tell them to use their prewriting plan from Lesson 27 or to brainstorm new ideas using Graphic Organizer 7.

Conference/Evaluate

During the writing process, circulate and help students select details to clearly explain the solution. Evaluate using the rubric on p. 104.

 Digital
- eBook
- WriteSmart
- Interactive Lessons

Problem/Solution Paragraph

A **problem/solution paragraph** introduces a problem and then explains a possible way to solve it.

Parts of a Problem/Solution Paragraph

- A topic sentence that tells the problem
- Supporting sentences that give a possible solution
- Details that explain the solution
- Ideas that are explained in a logical order

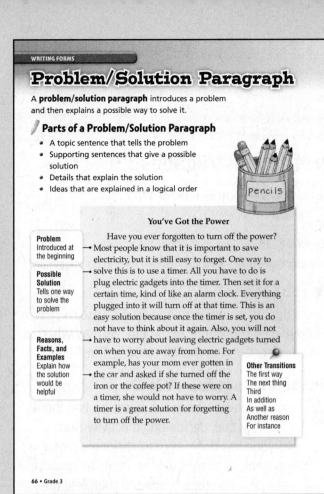

You've Got the Power

Problem
Introduced at the beginning

Possible Solution
Tells one way to solve the problem

Reasons, Facts, and Examples
Explain how the solution would be helpful

Have you ever forgotten to turn off the power? Most people know that it is important to save electricity, but it is still easy to forget. One way to solve this is to use a timer. All you have to do is plug electric gadgets into the timer. Then set it for a certain time, kind of like an alarm clock. Everything plugged into it will turn off at that time. This is an easy solution because once the timer is set, you do not have to think about it again. Also, you will not have to worry about leaving electric gadgets turned on when you are away from home. For example, has your mom ever gotten in the car and asked if she turned off the iron or the coffee pot? If these were on a timer, she would not have to worry. A timer is a great solution for forgetting to turn off the power.

Other Transitions
The first way
The next thing
Third
In addition
As well as
Another reason
For instance

Name _____

Follow your teacher's directions to complete the frame.

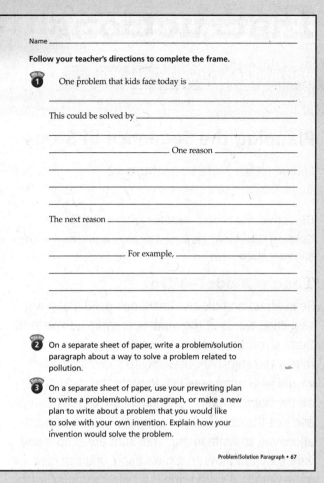

1 One problem that kids face today is _____

This could be solved by _____

_____. One reason _____

The next reason _____

_____. For example, _____

2 On a separate sheet of paper, write a problem/solution paragraph about a way to solve a problem related to pollution.

3 On a separate sheet of paper, use your prewriting plan to write a problem/solution paragraph, or make a new plan to write about a problem that you would like to solve with your own invention. Explain how your invention would solve the problem.

Corrective Feedback

IF . . . students are having difficulty writing a strong beginning,

THEN . . . have them consider ways the problem may impact readers. Explain that readers are more likely to be interested if they can connect the problem to their own lives. Students can use this connection to write a strong beginning. For example, *Have you ever spent the morning wondering whether or not you turned off the toaster oven? If so, a timer may be a great solution to your problem.*

Focus Trait: Ideas

Remind students that good writers elaborate with details to tell more about the solution, explain their ideas, and help readers clearly understand why the solution will work.

Write: *Picking up things to recycle or reuse helps the environment.* Explain that adding details could tell what things to recycle and reuse. Write: *Consistently picking up newspaper, soda cans, and plastic water bottles from parks and beaches helps the environment because it cleans up trash and allows us to reuse materials.*

Have students suggest details to elaborate on the following sentence: *We recycle paper.* Write their suggestions on the board, such as *Our class collects newspaper, homework pages, and worksheets to recycle and reuse.*

Grade 3 • **67**

Instructions

Minilesson 55

Planning the Sequence of Steps

Common Core State Standard: W.3.2

Objective: Plan how to organize instructions.

Guiding Question: How can I organize instructions to show the order of the steps?

Teach/Model—I Do

Read aloud and discuss handbook p. 68. Point out sequence words in the model paragraph. Explain that these show the order in which the reader must follow the steps. Another way to show the order would be a numbered list. Rewrite the instructions on the board as a list, including only the basic steps and not the details and examples. Explain that lists allow you to write instructions that are simple and very easy to follow. In a paragraph, you can give more details. A paragraph is a better form for instructions that describe a complicated task.

Guided Practice—We Do

Have students name projects with multiple steps, such as building a snowman or making a sandwich. Write topics on the board as students suggest them. Continue until you have a list of at least three topics. Together, choose one topic and list the first two steps. Then write those steps in paragraph form.

Practice/Apply—You Do

COLLABORATIVE Tell small groups to complete the list of steps. Then have them use sequence words to write the steps in paragraph form.

INDEPENDENT Instruct students to choose a new topic. Have them write the first three steps of the process in a numbered list. Then tell them to write the steps in paragraph form, using sequence words.

Conference/Evaluate

Circulate and help students think of sequence words to include in their paragraphs. Encourage them to refer to the Other Transitions list in the handbook.

Minilesson 56

Drafting Instructions

Common Core State Standard: W.3.2

Objective: Write clear instructions for a process.

Guiding Question: How do I explain how to do something?

Teach/Model—I Do

Have students review handbook p. 68. Discuss how the boldfaced transitions in the model show when to do each step. Go over the list of Other Transitions.

Guided Practice—We Do

 Have students turn to the frame on handbook p. 69. Together, decide on an activity that everyone has done, such as making a diorama or playing a game. Guide students to suggest materials and steps needed to complete the activity. List their ideas. Use the list to help students create sentences to complete the steps in sequential order. Have students write in their books as you write on the board.

Practice/Apply—You Do

 COLLABORATIVE Have small groups work together to write instructions for Activity 2 in which they choose and write about another topic. Have groups share their writing.

INDEPENDENT Have students read the directions. Tell them to use their prewriting plan from Lesson 28 or to brainstorm new ideas using Graphic Organizer 4.

Conference/Evaluate

During the writing process, circulate and offer encouragement and help as needed. Evaluate using the rubric on p. 104.

WriteSmart CD-ROM
Instructions (Process)

- eBook
- WriteSmart
- Interactive Lessons

Instructions

Instructions teach the reader how to do or make something. They give all the steps the reader must follow.

Parts of Instructions

- A topic sentence that tells what the instructions will explain
- A sentence stating all of the materials and supplies needed
- Words that show the order of the steps
- Exact words and details that explain each step
- A closing sentence that tells why the instructions are important or useful

Topic Sentence
Introduces the main idea

Materials
Tell everything the reader needs

Order Words
Show the order in which the steps should be followed

Closing Sentence
Tells why the instructions are useful and fun

Have you ever wished for a snowstorm even when it's warm outside? Here is how to make snowflakes you can keep inside all year. You will need white paper and scissors. **First**, fold the paper in half several times. Fold it any way you like. You can fold it up and down, sideways, or corner to corner. **Then** use scissors to cut lots of shapes from each side. Cut different shapes, such as squares, diamonds, and squiggles. Be sure not to cut away all the folds. You will need some folded parts to hold the paper together. **After** you cut, open the paper. It will look like a lacy snowflake. Hang it anywhere you like. Make a few more and you will feel like you live in a big snow globe!

Other Transitions
The first thing
Second
Next
Once that is done
After a while
Following this
Third
Last

Name _____

Follow your teacher's directions to complete the frame.

1 Something that is a lot of fun to do is _____
_____. You will need _____
_____. First, _____
_____
_____
_____
_____
_____
_____ Then _____
_____
_____. After _____
_____
_____
_____
_____ Finally, _____
_____
_____

2 On a separate sheet of paper, give instructions for something that is easy to do or make. Remember to include any materials you may need.

3 On a separate sheet of paper, use your prewriting plan to write instructions, or make a new plan to write instructions that explain something else you like to do.

✓ Corrective Feedback

IF . . . students think they may have left out important steps in their instructions,

THEN . . . have them read their instructions to a partner. If possible, have the partners follow (or mimic following) the steps exactly as they are written. Writers will be able to see immediately any information they have failed to include.

Focus Trait: Word Choice

Read aloud the following sentences from the model:

Then use scissors to cut lots of shapes from each side. Cut different shapes, such as squares, diamonds, and squiggles.

Discuss how exact words and details make the instructions clear for the reader.

Tell the class to draw a funny animal. Have students compare their drawings. Point out that the drawings are all quite different.

Then tell students to draw a chubby pink piglet rolling happily in the mud. Compare pictures again, pointing out that these drawings all look a lot more alike or at least have similar elements.

Explain that exact words and details give a clear idea of how to follow instructions.

Research Report: Prewriting

Minilesson 57

Choosing and Narrowing a Topic

Common Core State Standard: W.3.2a

Objective: Select a topic to research.

Guiding Question: What makes a good topic for a research report?

Teach/Model—I Do

Read and discuss handbook p. 70 with students. Point out that the writer first brainstormed a list of topics that she was interested in and then selected one to research. Explain that when writing a research report, writers should focus on specific ideas about the topic. For example, the writer of the student model narrowed her topic from basketball to the invention of basketball. One way to narrow a topic is to list several questions about it. Point out the questions in the model. Explain that these questions help the writer know what to look for when researching.

Guided Practice—We Do

Have students suggest several topics they might like to research, including people, places, sports, or events. Write their ideas on the board. Together, select a topic and elicit two or three questions about it. Repeat until you have worked together to narrow several of the topics.

Practice/Apply—You Do

COLLABORATIVE Tell small groups to select a different topic from the board and list several questions they have about it in order to narrow the topic for research.

INDEPENDENT Instruct students to choose a different topic from the board or to come up with their own and list several research questions to narrow the topic.

Conference/Evaluate

Circulate and help students narrow their topics. Encourage them to think about what they would like to learn about the topic.

Minilesson 58

Taking Notes

Common Core State Standards: W.3.2a, W.3.2b

Objective: Use notetaking strategies to record information.

Guiding Question: How do I take notes for a research report?

Teach/Model—I Do

Read aloud handbook p. 70. Point out facts in the model, such as *Dr. Naismith invented basketball*. Explain that the writer took notes to include these facts in the report. Writers look through sources, find facts, and write the most important facts and their sources on note cards. When they have enough facts to explain their topic, they organize the cards.

Guided Practice—We Do

 Have students turn to handbook p. 71. Help them list sports that could be the subject of a research report. Pick one, list questions about the topic, and discuss possible sources. Look up the topic in a book and read the facts aloud. Have students raise their hands when they hear a fact that answers one of the questions. Write each fact, source, and page number in a square to represent index cards. Have students write in their books as you write on the board.

Practice/Apply—You Do

 COLLABORATIVE Tell small groups to choose a topic for Activity 2. Give each group one source to find facts. Instruct students to find two facts and list them and their sources.

 INDEPENDENT Have students choose a topic for Activity 3 and find and write two facts.

Conference/Evaluate

During the writing process, circulate and help students take notes about a topic. Evaluate using the rubric on p. 104.

Digital
• eBook
• WriteSmart
• Interactive Lessons

Research Report: Prewriting

A **research report** uses facts from more than one source to explain a topic.

✏ Prewriting

* First, brainstorm a list of topics that interest you.
* Next, choose a topic that you would like to learn about. Use a graphic organizer to plan the questions you would like to answer, and organize the information that will be included in the report.

Topic brainstorming

France

Killer Whales

(Basketball)

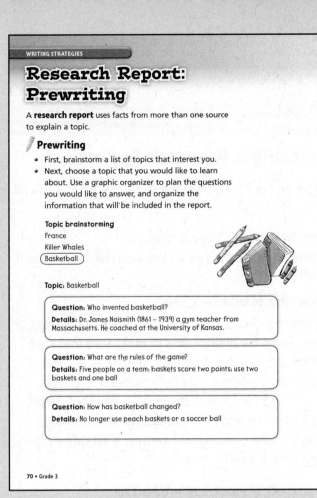

Topic: Basketball

> **Question:** Who invented basketball?
> **Details:** Dr. James Naismith (1861 – 1939) a gym teacher from Massachusetts. He coached at the University of Kansas.

> **Question:** What are the rules of the game?
> **Details:** Five people on a team; baskets score two points; use two baskets and one ball

> **Question:** How has basketball changed?
> **Details:** No longer use peach baskets or a soccer ball

Name _____

Follow your teacher's directions to complete this page.

1 **Topic:** The history of my favorite game _____

> Question:
>
> Details:

> Question:
>
> Details:

> Question:
>
> Details:

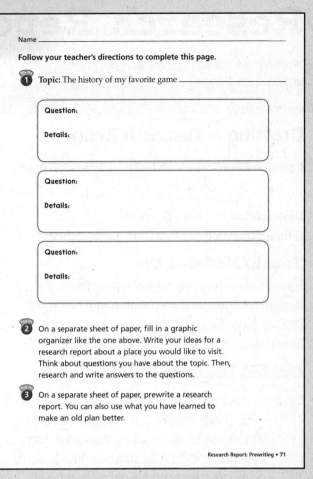

2 On a separate sheet of paper, fill in a graphic organizer like the one above. Write your ideas for a research report about a place you would like to visit. Think about questions you have about the topic. Then, research and write answers to the questions.

3 On a separate sheet of paper, prewrite a research report. You can also use what you have learned to make an old plan better.

✔ Corrective Feedback

IF . . . students are having difficulty selecting facts to include,

THEN . . . remind them that a research report will probably not be long enough to include all of the information about a topic. Writers must select only the most important facts and details to explain the topic and answer their questions. Guide students to only include the facts that clearly answer their research questions.

Focus Trait: Ideas

Remind students that good writers gather the most important ideas to include in a research report about a topic. They think about what they want to learn, select a main idea, and then use facts and details to support the main idea and answer their questions. Opinions are not included in a research report. Explain the difference between facts and opinions: facts can be proven, and opinions are someone's point of view.

Explain that when writers gather facts for a research report, they look in reliable sources such as encyclopedias, nonfiction books, magazines, and some Internet sites. They might also interview an expert on the topic. These sources can provide much information, and writers must select the most important facts to support the main idea and explain the topic.

Research Report

Minilesson 59

Drafting a Research Report

Common Core State Standards: W.3.2b, W.3.7, W.3.8

Objective: Write a research report.

Guiding Question: How do I draft a research report?

Teach/Model—I Do

Have students review the definition, Parts of a Research Report, and model on handbook p. 72. Discuss how the boldfaced words connect ideas and how the conclusion sums up the report.

Guided Practice—We Do

 Have students turn to the frame on handbook p. 73. Guide students to use their plans from Minilesson 58 to complete the frame. Remind students that copying someone else's words is called *plagiarism* and is not allowed. Help students sum up the main points of the report in the conclusion. Have students write in their books as you write on the board.

Practice/Apply—You Do

 COLLABORATIVE Have small groups work together to plan and write a research report for Activity 2 in which they use facts about another sport. Have groups share their writing.

 INDEPENDENT Have students read the directions. Tell them to use their prewriting plan from Lesson 30 or to brainstorm new ideas using Graphic Organizer 7.

Conference/Evaluate

During the writing process, circulate and offer encouragement and help as needed. Evaluate using the rubric on p. 104.

WriteSmart CD-ROM

Research Report

 Digital
• eBook
• WriteSmart
• Interactive Lessons

Minilesson 60

Revising a Research Report

Common Core State Standards: W.3.2, W.3.5, W.3.7, W.3.8

Objective: Revise a research report.

Guiding Question: How can I improve a draft of my research report?

Teach/Model—I Do

Review handbook p. 72. Tell students that one way they can revise their draft is to make sure that each paragraph includes clear topic sentences and detail sentences. Point out how the model accomplishes this. Suggest a detail that can be added for support, such as in the first body paragraph, *Dr. Naismith taught at the University of Kansas, where they have long, cold winters.*

Guided Practice—We Do

Have students turn to their drafts on handbook p. 73. Guide them to make sure the draft has clear topic sentences and supporting details. Help students remove unnecessary details and add details if needed. Remind students to use their own words when revising.

Practice/Apply—You Do

COLLABORATIVE Have small groups work together to revise Activity 2 on handbook p. 73. Remind them to add and subtract details as needed and check for clear topic sentences.

INDEPENDENT Have students revise their individual drafts, checking for clear topic sentences and strong supporting details.

Conference/Evaluate

Circulate and help students add interesting details and remove unnecessary ones.

Research Report

A **research report** uses facts to explain a topic. It is made up of several paragraphs with details that come from more than one source.

Parts of a Research Report

- An introduction that tells or asks something interesting about the topic
- A body made up of one or more paragraphs
- A topic sentence and details for each paragraph
- A conclusion that sums up the report
- A list of sources you used

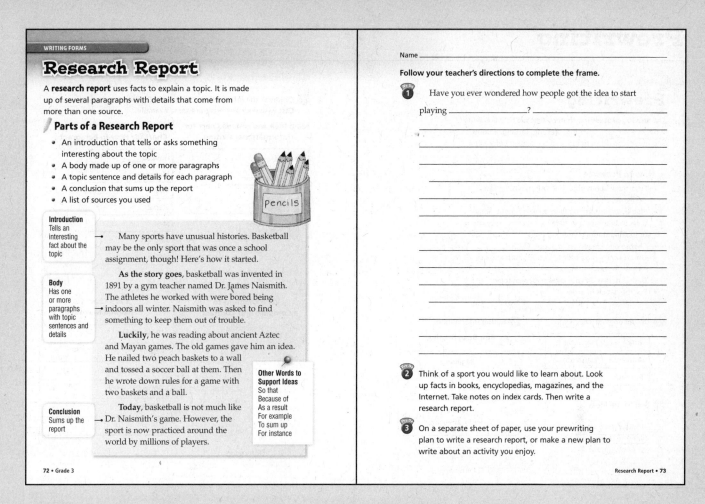

Introduction
Tells an interesting fact about the topic

> Many sports have unusual histories. Basketball may be the only sport that was once a school assignment, though! Here's how it started.

Body
Has one or more paragraphs with topic sentences and details

> **As the story goes**, basketball was invented in 1891 by a gym teacher named Dr. James Naismith. The athletes he worked with were bored being indoors all winter. Naismith was asked to find something to keep them out of trouble.

> **Luckily**, he was reading about ancient Aztec and Mayan games. The old games gave him an idea. He nailed two peach baskets to a wall and tossed a soccer ball at them. Then he wrote down rules for a game with two baskets and a ball.

Other Words to Support Ideas
So that
Because of
As a result
For example
To sum up
For instance

Conclusion
Sums up the report

> **Today**, basketball is not much like Dr. Naismith's game. However, the sport is now practiced around the world by millions of players.

72 • Grade 3

Name _____

Follow your teacher's directions to complete the frame.

 Have you ever wondered how people got the idea to start

playing _____? _____

_____

_____

_____

_____

_____

_____

_____

_____

_____

_____

_____

 Think of a sport you would like to learn about. Look up facts in books, encyclopedias, magazines, and the Internet. Take notes on index cards. Then write a research report.

3 On a separate sheet of paper, use your prewriting plan to write a research report, or make a new plan to write about an activity you enjoy.

Research Report • 73

✓ Corrective Feedback

IF . . . students are having trouble taking notes on their topic,

THEN . . . remind them that notes do not have to be in complete sentences. Tell students that they can restate their notes in complete sentences when they draft the report. Remind students to write down the source of each fact. That way, they will be able to check the facts or find additional information later.

Focus Trait: Organization

Point out the organization of the report on handbook p. 72: it has an introduction, a body, and a conclusion.

Then explain that the first sentence in the body paragraph is its topic sentence; it tells the main idea of the paragraph. The other sentences in the paragraph explain or support the main idea.

Ask students to state a fact from the body paragraph and tell how it supports the topic sentence.

Write a new topic sentence and have students suggest sentences that would support it.

Example topic sentence: *Four-legged animals can be found all over the world.*

Example supporting sentence: *Different kinds of deer, for example, live on five of the world's continents.*

Prewriting

Prewriting

The **writing process** is a strategy that can help you write. It has five stages: prewriting, drafting, revising, editing, and publishing. **Prewriting** means planning before you write.

How to Prewrite

- First, think about your TAP. TAP stands for **Task**, **Audience**, and **Purpose**.
- Plan by brainstorming ideas to write about. Some ways to brainstorm include making lists, freewriting, or looking through your journal.
- Choose one idea to write about. Circle it.
- Use a graphic organizer to decide which ideas to include in your writing.
- Gather details on your chosen idea, or topic.
- Put the details in order.

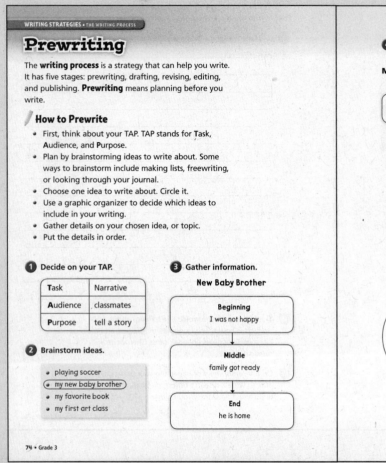

1. Decide on your TAP.

Task	Narrative
Audience	classmates
Purpose	tell a story

2. Brainstorm ideas.
- playing soccer
- my new baby brother
- my favorite book
- my first art class

3. Gather information.

New Baby Brother

Beginning
I was not happy

Middle
family got ready

End
he is home

4. **Organize the information.** Choose the Graphic Organizer that works best with your **TAP**. Here are some examples:

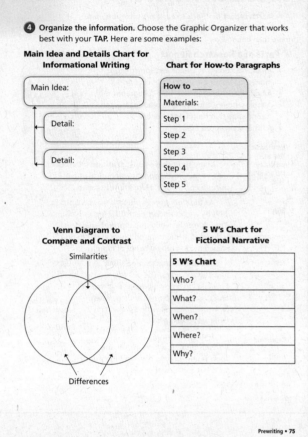

Main Idea and Details Chart for Informational Writing

Main Idea:

Detail:

Detail:

Chart for How-to Paragraphs

How to _____
Materials:
Step 1
Step 2
Step 3
Step 4
Step 5

Venn Diagram to Compare and Contrast

Similarities

Differences

5 W's Chart for Fictional Narrative

5 W's Chart
Who?
What?
When?
Where?
Why?

Minilesson 61

Introducing Prewriting

Common Core State Standard: W.3.5

Objective: Understand how to use the prewriting handbook pages.

Guiding Question: How do I plan which ideas to include in my writing?

Teach/Model

Have students read pp. 74–75. Explain that the example shows how a student planned a narrative essay by (1) thinking about the audience and purpose of the piece, (2) brainstorming possible topics, (3) listing ideas to include, and (4) organizing information.

Practice/Apply

Have students use the prewriting process to plan and organize a writing project of their own.

Minilesson 62

Organizing Ideas

Common Core State Standard: W.3.5

Objective: Organize ideas before writing.

Guiding Question: How do I choose the best order for the ideas in my writing?

Teach/Model

Explain that it is important to write ideas in a logical order. Point out that the ideas in the organizer on p. 74 are in time order because narratives usually tell a story from beginning to end.

Practice/Apply

Have students discuss what would be a logical order for the ideas in the organizers on p. 75. For example, informative essays state the main idea, followed by details that help to support or explain it.

Drafting

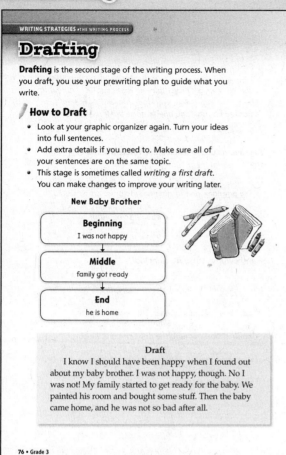

Drafting

Drafting is the second stage of the writing process. When you draft, you use your prewriting plan to guide what you write.

How to Draft

- Look at your graphic organizer again. Turn your ideas into full sentences.
- Add extra details if you need to. Make sure all of your sentences are on the same topic.
- This stage is sometimes called *writing a first draft*. You can make changes to improve your writing later.

New Baby Brother

Beginning
I was not happy

Middle
family got ready

End
he is home

Draft
I know I should have been happy when I found out about my baby brother. I was not happy, though. No I was not! My family started to get ready for the baby. We painted his room and bought some stuff. Then the baby came home, and he was not so bad after all.

76 • Grade 3

Topic: Raccoons

I. **Northern raccoons**
   a. Live in North and Central America
   b. Have thick, long gray fur
II. **Crab-eating raccoons**
   a. Live in Central and South America
   b. Have short, thin fur

Draft
There are two types of raccoons, northern raccoons and crab-eating raccoons. Northern raccoons live in North and Central America. They have thick, long gray fur. Crab-eating raccoons live in Central and South America. They have short, thin fur.

Opinion: Alice had a great adventure in Wonderland.

Reason: She changed sizes.

Reason: She could talk with animals.

Reason: She went to a party.

Draft
Alice had the most exciting adventure in Wonderland. First, she changed sizes. She got so small she couldn't reach the table! She found out she could talk to animals. Also, she went to a fun party.

Drafting • 77

WRITING STRATEGY

Minilesson 63

Introducing Drafting

Common Core State Standard: W.3.4

Objective: Understand how to use the drafting handbook pages.

Guiding Question: How do I use my prewriting plan to begin writing?

Teach/Model

Have students read pp. 76–77. Explain that the example on p. 76 shows how a student drafted a narrative from the organizer developed on p. 74 during the prewriting phase. Then discuss how the writers of the other examples drafted their pieces from ideas in different types of organizers.

Practice/Apply

Based on the outline on raccoons on p. 77, have students draft a concluding statement.

Minilesson 64

Developing Ideas in a Draft

Common Core State Standard: W.3.4

Objective: Understand that ideas in a graphic organizer can be changed when writing a draft.

Guiding Question: How do I turn my prewriting into a draft?

Teach/Model

Explain that a graphic organizer is like an outline and that writers often add or change ideas and information as they draft. Point out the introduction, details, and transitions that were added to the second draft on p. 76.

Practice/Apply

Have students discuss differences between the organizers and drafts on p. 77 (ex: an introductory sentence was added to both drafts; *great adventure* was changed to *most exciting adventure*).

Writing for Common Core • 75

Revising

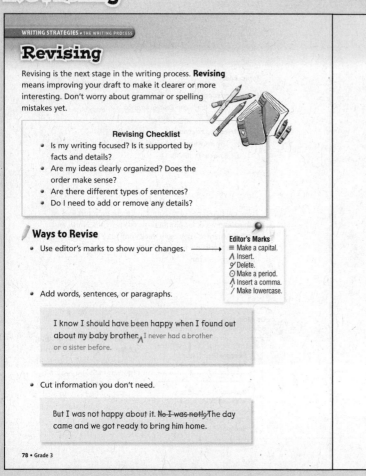

Revising

Revising is the next stage in the writing process. **Revising** means improving your draft to make it clearer or more interesting. Don't worry about grammar or spelling mistakes yet.

Revising Checklist
- Is my writing focused? Is it supported by facts and details?
- Are my ideas clearly organized? Does the order make sense?
- Are there different types of sentences?
- Do I need to add or remove any details?

Ways to Revise
- Use editor's marks to show your changes. →

Editor's Marks
≡ Make a capital.
∧ Insert.
ℐ Delete.
⊙ Make a period.
∧ Insert a comma.
/ Make lowercase.

- Add words, sentences, or paragraphs.

> I know I should have been happy when I found out about my baby brother. ∧ I never had a brother or a sister before.

- Cut information you don't need.

> But I was not happy about it. No I was not! The day came and we got ready to bring him home.

78 • Grade 3

- Replace information with something new or better.

> But I was not happy about it. No I was not! The day came and we got ready to bring him home. We painted his room and bought some stuff. ∧ toys, diapers, and bottles.

- Move information so that it is in an order that makes sense.

> The day came and we got ready to bring him home. We painted his room and bought some stuff. ∧ toys, diapers, and bottles.

Here's how a revised draft might look:

> I know I should have been happy when I found out about my baby brother. But I was not happy about it. No I was not! I never had a brother or sister before. The day came and we got ready to bring him home. We painted his room and bought some stuff. ∧ toys, diapers, and bottles.

Revising • 79

Minilesson 65

Introducing Revising

Common Core State Standard: W.3.5

Objective: Understand how to revise a draft.

Guiding Question: What changes could improve my writing?

Teach/Model

Read and discuss pp. 78–79. Tell students that asking themselves the questions in the checklist can help them identify ways to make their writing better. Point out and discuss changes that the student made to improve the draft. Emphasize that the writer added information that helped explain the ideas and also removed a sentence that was not needed.

Practice/Apply

Review pp. 78–79. Then have volunteers reread the last draft on p. 79.

Minilesson 66

Using Editor's Marks

Common Core State Standard: W.3.5

Objective: Understand how to use editor's marks to revise.

Guiding Question: How do I show what changes should be made to my draft?

Teach/Model

Remind students that a draft is often called the *sloppy copy* and that it is not always necessary to erase to make changes. Review the editor's marks on p. 78. Discuss how each mark is used to show a change that will improve the draft.

Practice/Apply

Have students identify editor's marks used in the drafts on pp. 78–79. Discuss the changes that are indicated by each mark.

Editing and Publishing

Editing

Editing is the stage of the writing process that follows revision. During this stage, you find and fix mistakes.

Editing

- Check for mistakes in punctuation, capitalization, spelling, and grammar.
- Make sure your paragraphs are indented.
- Use editor's marks to fix your writing.
- Use the spelling and grammar checker if you are working on a computer. Be sure to double-check your work for errors the checker won't catch.

Editor's Marks
≡ Make a capital.
∧ Insert.
⌿ Delete.
⊙ Make a period.
∧ Insert a comma.
/ Make lowercase.

Revised Draft

Carrie wanted a puppy. Instead, her mom and dad said she would soon have a baby sister. Carrie was not happy. Puppies were more fun than babies. But on the day the baby came home, Carrie looked at the pink bundle and fell in love.

Publishing

The last stage of the writing process is **publishing**, or sharing your writing with others. Before you publish, you can go back to any stage to improve your writing.

- Decide how you want to publish. You can share a written piece or give a presentation to your class.
- Type or write a clean copy of your piece.
- When you give a presentation, use note cards with the main ideas to guide you.

Jasper, My New Baby Brother

I know I should have been happy when I found out about my baby brother. I was not happy, though. I had never had a brother or sister before. We painted his room and bought some toys, diapers, and bottles. Dad let me help him put the crib together.

The day came, and we brought him home. Now that Jasper is home, I know he is a lot of fun. He smiles when I rock him, and he laughs and makes funny noises. I love my baby brother!

WRITING STRATEGY

Minilesson 67

Introducing Editing

Common Core State Standard: W.3.5

Objective: Understand how to edit a draft.
Guiding Question: How do I fix mistakes in my writing?

Teach/Model

Read and discuss p. 80. Explain that students can use a checklist similar to the one on this page to identify errors in their drafts. Remind students that computer spelling checkers do not recognize all mistakes; they often miss such errors as incorrect homonyms (for example, *know / no*) or misspellings that are words (*not* for *note*).

Practice/Apply

Have students identify corrections the writer made to the model and explain the editor's marks used.

Minilesson 68

Introducing Publishing

Common Core State Standard: W.3.5

Objective: Understand how to publish a piece of writing.
Guiding Question: How can I share my writing with others?

Teach/Model

Read p. 81 together. Point out that the final copy is error free and that the changes the writer would have indicated during editing have been made. Explain that the writer went back to the revision stage to make improvements; point out those changes (added a title, reworded *But I was not happy…*, added details and conclusion).

Practice/Apply

Review the many ways to publish, from writing to making multimedia presentations; discuss why a writer might choose each one.

Writing for Common Core • 77

Ideas

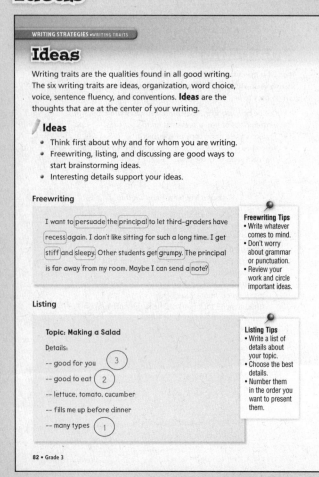

Ideas

Writing traits are the qualities found in all good writing. The six writing traits are ideas, organization, word choice, voice, sentence fluency, and conventions. **Ideas** are the thoughts that are at the center of your writing.

Ideas

- Think first about why and for whom you are writing.
- Freewriting, listing, and discussing are good ways to start brainstorming ideas.
- Interesting details support your ideas.

Freewriting

I want to persuade the principal to let third-graders have recess again. I don't like sitting for such a long time. I get stiff and sleepy. Other students get grumpy. The principal is far away from my room. Maybe I can send a note?

Freewriting Tips
- Write whatever comes to mind.
- Don't worry about grammar or punctuation.
- Review your work and circle important ideas.

Listing

Topic: Making a Salad

Details:

-- good for you 3

-- good to eat 2

-- lettuce, tomato, cucumber

-- fills me up before dinner

-- many types 1

Listing Tips
- Write a list of details about your topic.
- Choose the best details.
- Number them in the order you want to present them.

Narrative Writing
- For a personal narrative, list events and details you remember.
- For a fictional story, brainstorm about characters, plot, and setting.
- Good graphic organizers for ideas: story map, 5 Ws chart

Who?	Diego and Sonia
What?	collected pennies for charity
When?	in September
Where?	at school
Why?	to help build schools in poorer countries

Informative Writing
- List what you already know about your topic, then do research.
- Good graphic organizers for ideas: web, note cards, timeline

Redwood trees are one of the oldest living things on earth.

-- can grow more than 350 feet tall

-- live for more than 1,000 years

Source: Kids Nature Magazine

Persuasive Writing
- Write your goal or opinion. Make a list of your thoughts and feelings.
- Research facts to support your goal or opinion.
- Good graphic organizers for ideas: idea-support map, column chart

Recycling		
reason: helps the environment	**reason:** protects animals and plants	**reason:** saves money
detail: easy to do	**detail:** animals can eat plastic and get sick	**detail:** good to use things again
detail: creates less pollution		**detail:** bottles, cans, paper

---

Minilesson 69

Introducing Ideas

Common Core State Standard: W.3.5

Objective: Recognize ideas as the center of writing.

Guiding Question: What ideas should be used in my writing?

Teach/Model

Read and discuss p. 82. Explain that writing is made up of ideas that support the writer's reason for writing and are interesting to the audience. Point out that the purpose of the first sample is to persuade and that the ideas in it are intended to convince the audience to agree with the writer's goal.

Practice/Apply

Have students identify the topic or purpose of the freewriting and the listing.

Minilesson 70

Generating Ideas

Common Core State Standard: W.3.5

Objective: Understand strategies for generating ideas.

Guiding Question: How can I get ideas to include in writing?

Teach/Model

Read p. 83 together. Review the organizers on the page. On the board, invite volunteers to draw an example of a story map, web, vertical timeline, and idea-support map.

Practice/Apply

Have small groups work together to generate ideas to add to one of the models on pp. 82–83. Remind students to write anything that comes to mind.

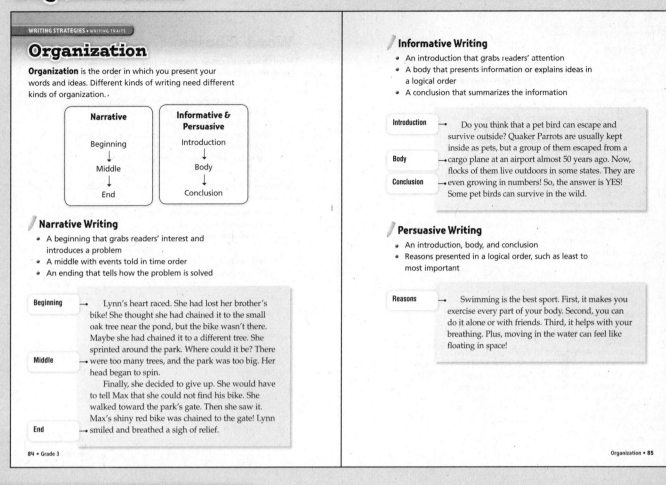

Organization

WRITING STRATEGIES • WRITING TRAITS

Organization

Organization is the order in which you present your words and ideas. Different kinds of writing need different kinds of organization.

Narrative

Beginning
↓
Middle
↓
End

Informative & Persuasive

Introduction
↓
Body
↓
Conclusion

Narrative Writing

- A beginning that grabs readers' interest and introduces a problem
- A middle with events told in time order
- An ending that tells how the problem is solved

Beginning → Lynn's heart raced. She had lost her brother's bike! She thought she had chained it to the small oak tree near the pond, but the bike wasn't there. Maybe she had chained it to a different tree. She sprinted around the park. Where could it be? There

Middle → were too many trees, and the park was too big. Her head began to spin.

Finally, she decided to give up. She would have to tell Max that she could not find his bike. She walked toward the park's gate. Then she saw it! Max's shiny red bike was chained to the gate! Lynn

End → smiled and breathed a sigh of relief.

Informative Writing

- An introduction that grabs readers' attention
- A body that presents information or explains ideas in a logical order
- A conclusion that summarizes the information

Introduction → Do you think that a pet bird can escape and survive outside? Quaker Parrots are usually kept inside as pets, but a group of them escaped from a

Body → cargo plane at an airport almost 50 years ago. Now, flocks of them live outdoors in some states. They are

Conclusion → even growing in numbers! So, the answer is YES! Some pet birds can survive in the wild.

Persuasive Writing

- An introduction, body, and conclusion
- Reasons presented in a logical order, such as least to most important

Reasons → Swimming is the best sport. First, it makes you exercise every part of your body. Second, you can do it alone or with friends. Third, it helps with your breathing. Plus, moving in the water can feel like floating in space!

WRITING STRATEGY

Minilesson 71

Introducing Organization

Common Core State Standard: W.3.4

Objective: Recognize organization of various writing forms.

Guiding Question: How should my ideas be organized?

Teach/Model

Read and discuss pp. 84–85. Point out the organization of each writing form. Explain that narrative writing usually organizes events according to what happens in the beginning, middle, and end. Informative and persuasive writing organize by introduction, a body with supporting details, and a conclusion.

Practice/Apply

Have students identify story elements in the model (characters, setting, problem, and so on).

Minilesson 72

Using Logical Order

Common Core State Standard: W.3.4

Objective: Recognize ways to organize information.

Guiding Question: What order of ideas is most logical?

Teach/Model

Review p. 85 together. Point out that, in informative and persuasive writing, facts are presented in a logical order. Explain that this order can be most to least important, least to most important, strongest to weakest evidence or *vice versa*, or stating information in time order. Note that writers choose the order that is most effective for the purpose of the writing.

Practice/Apply

Discuss how the writers ordered information in the sample paragraphs and why the order is effective.

Voice and Word Choice

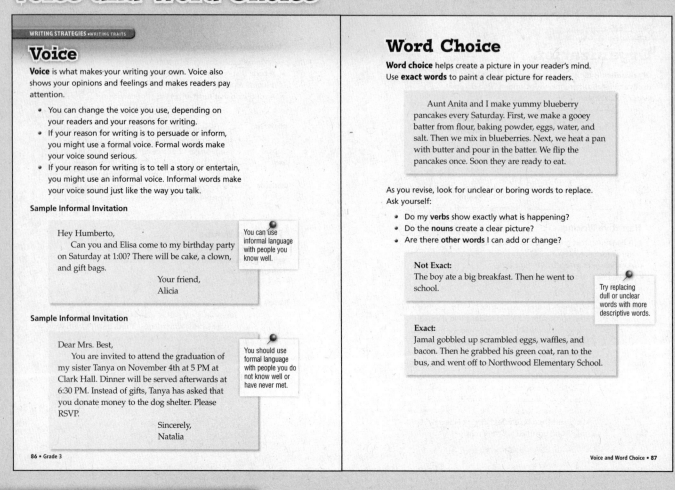

Voice

Voice is what makes your writing your own. Voice also shows your opinions and feelings and makes readers pay attention.

- You can change the voice you use, depending on your readers and your reasons for writing.
- If your reason for writing is to persuade or inform, you might use a formal voice. Formal words make your voice sound serious.
- If your reason for writing is to tell a story or entertain, you might use an informal voice. Informal words make your voice sound just like the way you talk.

Sample Informal Invitation

> Hey Humberto,
>   Can you and Elisa come to my birthday party on Saturday at 1:00? There will be cake, a clown, and gift bags.
>
>   Your friend,
>   Alicia

You can use informal language with people you know well.

Sample Informal Invitation

> Dear Mrs. Best,
>   You are invited to attend the graduation of my sister Tanya on November 4th at 5 PM at Clark Hall. Dinner will be served afterwards at 6:30 PM. Instead of gifts, Tanya has asked that you donate money to the dog shelter. Please RSVP.
>
>   Sincerely,
>   Natalia

You should use formal language with people you do not know well or have never met.

Word Choice

Word choice helps create a picture in your reader's mind. Use **exact words** to paint a clear picture for readers.

> Aunt Anita and I make yummy blueberry pancakes every Saturday. First, we make a gooey batter from flour, baking powder, eggs, water, and salt. Then we mix in blueberries. Next, we heat a pan with butter and pour in the batter. We flip the pancakes once. Soon they are ready to eat.

As you revise, look for unclear or boring words to replace. Ask yourself:

- Do my **verbs** show exactly what is happening?
- Do the **nouns** create a clear picture?
- Are there **other words** I can add or change?

Not Exact:
The boy ate a big breakfast. Then he went to school.

Try replacing dull or unclear words with more descriptive words.

Exact:
Jamal gobbled up scrambled eggs, waffles, and bacon. Then he grabbed his green coat, ran to the bus, and went off to Northwood Elementary School.

WRITING STRATEGY

Minilesson 73

Introducing Voice

Common Core State Standard: W.3.10

Objective: Recognize how voice is used in writing.
Guiding Question: What voice should be used for various types of writing?

Teach/Model

Read p. 86 together. Explain that a writer's voice changes, depending on the audience and purpose of the piece that is being written. Relate this to how students would not use the same words and tone with the principal as with a friend.

Practice/Apply

Have students point out differences between formal and informal language in the models. Discuss how the writer's voice is different in each example.

Minilesson 74

Introducing Word Choice

Common Core State Standard: W.3.10

Objective: Understand how word choice impacts writing.
Guiding Question: How can using exact words help readers better understand what I write?

Teach/Model

Read and discuss p. 87. Point out exact words and phrases that give readers a clear understanding of the event and make the writing more interesting *(blueberry, gooey, flip the pancakes once).*

Practice/Apply

Have students discuss why the *Exact* model is clearer than the *Not Exact* model. Then ask small groups to use different exact words and phrases to revise the *Not Exact* model.

Sentence Fluency

Sentence Fluency

Sentence fluency means that a writer's sentences flow smoothly. Fluent sentences make writers want to keep reading.

- Use different kinds of sentences.
- Combine choppy sentences into longer, smoother ones.
- Use a variety of sentence beginnings.
- Create different sentence lengths.
- Connect ideas from sentence to sentence.
- Make sure sentences are in the right order.

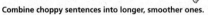

Combine choppy sentences into longer, smoother ones.

Choppy Sentences	Combine into longer, smoother ones
My brother got a new cat. The cat's name is Max.	My brother got a new cat whose name is Max.
Grandma likes to rake the leaves. The leaves fall in her garden.	Grandma likes to rake the leaves that fall in her garden.
Jackson read the book. It was about snakes.	Jackson read the book about snakes.

Use a variety of sentence beginnings.

Too Many Sentences Beginning the Same Way	Variety of Sentence Beginnings
Ron grabbed his backpack. He put his lucky baseball mitt inside. He checked his backpack one last time. He called to his mother, "I'm ready for the game!"	Ron grabbed his backpack. Then he put his lucky baseball mitt inside. After checking his backpack one last time, he called to his mother, "I'm ready for the game!"

88 • Grade 3

Create different sentence lengths.

Too Many Sentences of the Same Length	Varied Lengths
Jawara called his sister. He asked to borrow her computer. He had a project to do. He went to her room. He turned the computer on. He waited for it to start up. He said, "This computer is taking forever."	Jawara called his sister. He asked to borrow her computer because he had a project to do. When he got to her room, he turned the computer on. After waiting a few minutes for it to start up, he thought, "This computer is taking forever."

Connect ideas from sentence to sentence. Make sure they are in the right order.

Unconnected ideas	Connected ideas
Carnivals have been entertaining people for a long time. We have never had one in our city. It had a lot of games and food and rides, and I like the games best. I won a stuffed giraffe! There was a contest to guess how many pennies were in a jar. A carnival was here for two weeks in the summer.	Carnivals have been entertaining people for a long time, but we have never had one in our city before. One finally came here for two weeks in the summer. It had a lot of games, food, and rides. I like games the best. There was a contest to guess how many pennies were in a jar, and I won a stuffed giraffe!

Sentence Fluency • 89

WRITING STRATEGY

Minilesson 75

Introducing Sentence Fluency

Common Core State Standard: W.3.5

Objective: Recognize how sentence fluency improves writing

Guiding Question: How can I make my writing flow smoothly?

Teach/Model

Read and discuss pp. 88–89. Review the list of strategies for improving fluency. Explain that the models show changes the writers made to help the writing flow more smoothly.

Practice/Apply

Have small groups compare the left- and right-hand models. Ask them to identify the changes shown in the right-hand models and discuss how these changes improved sentence fluency. Have groups share their ideas with the class.

Minilesson 76

Using Connecting Words

Common Core State Standard: W.3.5

Objective: Identify words that connect ideas in sentences

Guiding Question: What words can I use to connect ideas?

Teach/Model

Review the second pair of models on p. 88. Explain that connecting words show how ideas are related. Point out time-order words that connect ideas in the improved sentences (*then, after*). Explain that these words connect ideas and improve sentence fluency.

Practice/Apply

Have students identify connecting words that show relationships between the ideas on p. 89 (*because, after, but, and*). Explain that these words improve fluency by combining sentences and ideas.

Conventions

WRITING STRATEGIES • WRITING TRAITS

Conventions

Conventions are rules for grammar, spelling, punctuation, and capitalization. One way to make sure you are following the rules when you write or edit is to have an editing checklist.

Sample Editing Checklist

Punctuation
___ Did I use correct end punctuation in my sentences?
___ Did I use commas correctly in compound sentences?
___ Did I use quotation marks correctly?
Capitalization
___ Did I start every sentence with a capital letter?
___ Did I capitalize proper nouns?
Spelling
___ Did I spell all of my words correctly?
Grammar
___ Did my sentences have correct subject-verb agreement?
___ Did I avoid sentence fragments?

Common Errors

Sentence Fragments
A sentence should have both a subject and a verb.

Wrong Way	Right Way
A leaf from a tree.	The leaf fell from the tree.
Because autumn is coming.	I feel happy because autumn is coming.
Piles of leaves on the ground to jump in.	Soon, there will be piles of leaves on the ground to jump in.

90 • Grade 3

Common and Proper Nouns
Most nouns are **common nouns**. These are general people, places, or things, and are not capitalized. A **proper noun** names a specific person, place, or thing. Proper nouns are always capitalized.

Wrong Way	Right Way
I talked to the Teacher about my vacation.	I talked to the teacher about my vacation.
Then mrs. morris told me about her trip to mexico.	Then Mrs. Morris told me about her trip to Mexico.

Subject-Verb Agreement
Make sure the subject and verb of your sentence agree.

Wrong Way	Right Way
Mario eat pizza on Saturdays.	Mario eats pizza on Saturdays.
Terri and Lucia runs to the corner and back every day.	Terri and Lucia run to the corner and back every day.

Correct use of commas in sentences
When you list three or more items in a sentence, it is called a **series**. Put commas between items in a series. Use a comma to combine two sentences into one compound sentence.

Wrong Way	Right Way
My new hat was green red and blue.	My new hat was green, red, and blue.
Annie came for a visit, I wasn't home.	Annie came for a visit, but I wasn't home.

Conventions • 91

Minilesson 77

Introducing Conventions

Common Core State Standard: W.3.5

Objective: Understand rules for conventions.

Guiding Question: What conventions should I check for when editing?

Teach/Model

Read and discuss pp. 90–91. Review the editing checklist and explain that good writers check their work for these items and then make any corrections that are needed.

Practice/Apply

Have students read the explanation and examples of common errors. Discuss what is wrong with each example on the left and how it was corrected to the right.

Minilesson 78

Capitalizing of Proper Nouns

Common Core State Standard: W.3.5

Objective: Identify and capitalize proper nouns.

Guiding Question: How do I recognize which words are proper nouns?

Teach/Model

Review the explanation of common and proper nouns on p. 91. Point out that *teacher* is a common noun and *Mrs. Morris* is a proper noun.

Practice/Apply

Have students identify the errors under "Wrong Way" and discuss the corrections made under "Right Way" on p. 91.

Writing Workshop

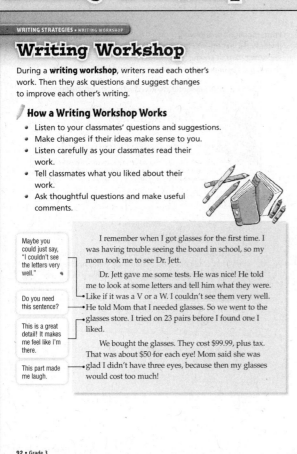

Writing Workshop

During a **writing workshop**, writers read each other's work. Then they ask questions and suggest changes to improve each other's writing.

How a Writing Workshop Works

- Listen to your classmates' questions and suggestions.
- Make changes if their ideas make sense to you.
- Listen carefully as your classmates read their work.
- Tell classmates what you liked about their work.
- Ask thoughtful questions and make useful comments.

Maybe you could just say, "I couldn't see the letters very well."

Do you need this sentence?

This is a great detail! It makes me feel like I'm there.

This part made me laugh.

I remember when I got glasses for the first time. I was having trouble seeing the board in school, so my mom took me to see Dr. Jett.

Dr. Jett gave me some tests. He was nice! He told me to look at some letters and tell him what they were. Like if it was a V or a W. I couldn't see them very well. He told Mom that I needed glasses. So we went to the glasses store. I tried on 23 pairs before I found one I liked.

We bought the glasses. They cost $99.99, plus tax. That was about $50 for each eye! Mom said she was glad I didn't have three eyes, because then my glasses would cost too much!

Tips for a Workshop

Sharing your writing will help you improve your work and find mistakes you did not see. Helping others with their writing also helps you find ways to fix your own writing.

During Prewriting
Working with others can help you…

- brainstorm topics to write about.
- find information about your topic.

As You Review Your First Draft
Working with others can tell you…

- what they liked.
- what parts they have questions about.

As You Revise
Working with others can tell you if…

- the beginning gets their interest.
- the middle part sticks to the topic.
- the ending is strong.

As You Edit and Proofread
Working with others can help you…

- check your capitalization.
- check your punctuation.
- check your spelling.

WRITING STRATEGY

Minilesson 79

Introducing Writing Workshop

Common Core State Standard: W.3.5

Objective: Understand the purpose of a writing workshop.

Guiding Question: What happens during a writing workshop?

Teach/Model

Read p. 92 together. Explain that the page shows a student's writing and that the boxes to the side show the questions and comments shared by the writer's classmates. Point out that the comments are specific, polite, and helpful, not nasty, rude, or just critical.

Practice/Apply

Tell students to suppose the model was a piece of writing that a classmate shared with them. Discuss additional questions or comments they might have about the story.

Minilesson 80

Using Tips During a Writing Workshop

Common Core State Standard: W.3.5

Objective: Recognize ways a writing workshop is beneficial.

Guiding Question: How can I improve my work by sharing it?

Teach/Model

Read and discuss p. 93. Explain that, for writers, working with others is beneficial because writers often overlook their own mistakes and may not recognize when their writing is unclear. Discuss how working with others can be helpful in each stage of the writing process.

Practice/Apply

Have students work with a partner to read a sample of each other's work, ask questions, and make suggestions for improvement.

Using the Internet

TECHNOLOGY

Using the Internet

The Internet is a great place to find information. Once you have a topic to research, you can search websites to answer your questions.

- A search engine will help you find websites about your topic. If you are not sure whether a particular website is a good source, ask your teacher.
- Many encyclopedias, dictionaries, magazines, and newspapers can be found online.
- Be sure to record your sources. When you take notes, write down the address, or the URL, of the website. Look for the author and the date.

Parts of a Website

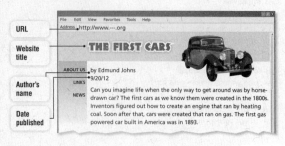

URL
Website title
Author's name
Date published

File Edit View Favorites Tools Help
Address http://www.---.org

THE FIRST CARS

ABOUT US by Edmund Johns
LINKS 9/20/12
NEWS Can you imagine life when the only way to get around was by horse-drawn car? The first cars as we know them were created in the 1800s. Inventors figured out how to create an engine that ran by heating coal. Soon after that, cars were created that ran on gas. The first gas powered car built in America was in 1893.

Print, Highlight, and Reword
If you find a website you like, you can highlight the important parts in another color. When you write your report, put the information in your own words.

File Edit View Favorites Tools Help
Address http://www.---.org

Flamingo Facts
by Christy Oiseau
May 7, 2012

Flamingos might just look like tall pink birds with really long legs, but they are much more than that. There are actually five species of flamingos. All are characterized by having long legs and necks, but they are not all pink. In fact, their colors include black, red, and yellow.

Flamingos
by Stacy Fiore

If you have seen a flamingo, you know it is a tall pink bird. That is just one kind of flamingo, though. There are actually five kinds of flamingos! They all have long necks and long legs, but not all are pink. Some flamingos are black, red, or yellow.

WRITING STRATEGY

Minilesson 81

Introducing Using the Internet

Common Core State Standards: W.3.7, W.3.8

Objective: Understand how to use the Internet for research.

Guiding Question: How can I find information on the Internet?

Teach/Model

Read and discuss p. 94. Point out that the illustration shows an Internet page on a computer screen. Discuss the parts of the website. Explain that URLs ending with *.edu* or *.org* are usually reliable sources of information.

Practice/Apply

Guide small groups to type research topics into a search engine and browse resulting web pages.

Minilesson 82

Restating Information from Sources

Common Core State Standard: W.3.8

Objective: Restate research information.

Guiding Question: How do I tell information in my own words?

Teach/Model

Read and discuss p. 95. Point out the circled information on the webpage and how the same facts have been restated, in the model, in the writer's own words.

Practice/Apply

Have students work with a partner to restate information from the webpage on p. 94. Have them share their statements with the class.

Writing for the Web

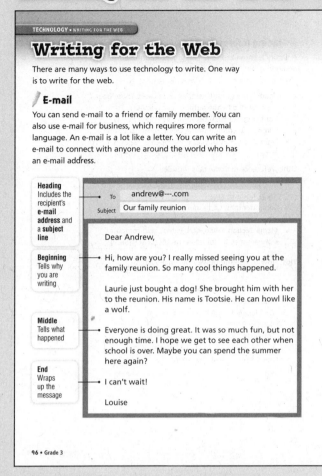

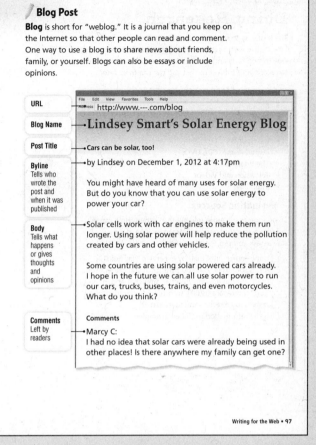

WRITING STRATEGY

Minilesson 83

Writing for the Web

Common Core State Standard: W.3.6

Objective: Understand how to write e-mails and blogs.
Guiding Question: How do I write e-mails and blogs?

Teach/Model

Read and discuss pp. 96–97. Explain that these are samples of an e-mail and a blog post written by students. Point out the boxes that tell what information to include in an e-mail.

Practice/Apply

Have students discuss similarities and differences between a written letter and an e-mail. Guide them to recognize that both have a greeting, body, and closing, but e-mails include an e-mail address, rather than a street address, and are delivered instantly.

Minilesson 84

Including Information in a Blog Post

Common Core State Standard: W.3.6

Objective: Recognize information to include in a weblog.
Guiding Question: What do I need to include in my blog?

Teach/Model

Review p. 97. Point out the information in the boxes along the left-hand side of the example. Explain that a blog is on-going and that the writer adds to it over a period of time. Point out the parts of a blog entry, including the name of the blog and the title of the post.

Practice/Apply

Have small groups write replies to the posted comment. Then have them write an entry for a new blog, including the blog name, title, byline, and body.

Writing for Common Core • 85

Doing Research

Doing Research

The best way to support your ideas in persuasive or informative writing is to use facts and details. The best way to find facts and details is to do research. Remember to record your sources so that you can cite them later.

Sources of Information

- Books
- Encyclopedias
- Magazines
- Newspapers
- Digital Audio, CDs, DVDs
- The Internet
- Television and Videos
- Interviews

Evaluating Sources

Some sources are more reliable than others. How can you tell which sources are good? When looking at a new source, ask yourself these questions:

- ☐ Is the source published by experts in that field?
- ☐ If it is a website, can you trust it? (If you are not sure, then you can ask your teacher. Sites that end in *.edu*, *.org*, or *.gov* are usually websites you can trust.)
- ☐ Is the source recent and up to date?
- ☐ Is the information useful and complete?

Finding Information

A library is organized to help you find information. The books in a library are divided into three main sections: Fiction, Nonfiction, and Reference Books.

- **Fiction** books include stories and novels. These books are arranged by the authors' last names.
- **Nonfiction** (factual) books are arranged by call numbers, according to the Dewey decimal system.
- **Reference** books such as encyclopedias, atlases, and dictionaries are kept in a special section of the library.

Other reference material may include:

- **Magazines** and **Newspapers**. These may be found in the periodicals area.
- **Computer labs**. Computers with connection to the Internet may be at your library.
- **Media Section**. DVDs, CDs, videos, and computer software may be found in the Media Section.

Tips: How to Use the Dewey Decimal System

- A book numbered **386** comes before a book numbered **714**
- One labeled **973A** comes before one labeled **973B**.
- Some call numbers have decimals, like **973.19** or **973.22**. Ask your librarian if you need help finding these books.

WRITING STRATEGY

Minilesson 85

Doing Research

Common Core State Standards: W.3.7, W.3.8

Objective: Recognize various sources for researching facts.

Guiding Question: Where can I find facts to support my ideas?

Teach/Model

Read and discuss p. 98. Discuss how, for many topics, new information is often discovered; sources should be as recent as possible. Facts about historic topics, however, do not change much, so publication dates are less important.

Practice/Apply

Have students suggest possible topics to research. Discuss the best sources to use to research each (ex: *upcoming local election: newspaper, interview with mayor; Abe Lincoln: encyclopedia, biography*).

Minilesson 86

Finding Information

Common Core State Standard: W.3.8

Objective: Understand how to find information in a library.

Guiding Question: Where can I find facts in the library?

Teach/Model

Review p. 99. Discuss how nonfiction and reference materials are used for research. Explain that the Dewey Decimal System groups similar books together. For example, geography and history books are given 900 numbers. This system is used in many libraries.

Practice/Apply

Have small groups select a topic to research. Then have them list the types of materials they would use to find information on that topic, as well as where they would look in the library to find the materials.

Notetaking

RESEARCH

Notetaking

You will find a lot of information when you research. One way to keep track of it and stay organized is to take notes.

Note Cards

You can take notes on your research in two ways.

1. You can write a main idea or a research question at the top of the card. Then write details or the answer to your research question below. At the bottom, be sure to include your source.

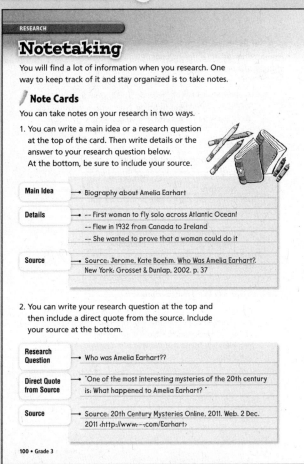

Main Idea	→	Biography about Amelia Earhart
Details	→	-- First woman to fly solo across Atlantic Ocean!
		-- Flew in 1932 from Canada to Ireland
		-- She wanted to prove that a woman could do it
Source	→	Source: Jerome, Kate Boehm. Who Was Amelia Earhart?. New York: Grosset & Dunlap, 2002. p. 37

2. You can write your research question at the top and then include a direct quote from the source. Include your source at the bottom.

Research Question	→	Who was Amelia Earhart??
Direct Quote from Source	→	"One of the most interesting mysteries of the 20th century is: What happened to Amelia Earhart?"
Source	→	Source: 20th Century Mysteries Online, 2011. Web. 2 Dec. 2011 <http://www.---.com/Earhart>

Writing to Learn

Think-Aloud on Paper
- As you read, list ideas you want to remember.
- Use diagrams, drawings, or graphic organizers to show how ideas connect.
- As you read, write questions in a journal or log. Later, research the answers to your questions, or ask your teacher for help.

Learning Logs
- A learning log is a place for you to comment on, ask questions about, or make connections to your reading.
- In the left column, **Note-Taking,** write the exact words you read.
- In the right column, **Note-Making,** write thoughts and questions about the notes in the left column.

Learning Log: "Amelia Disappears!"	
Note-Taking	Note-Making
"In June 1937, she left Miami, Florida, on an around-the-world flight attempt."	Was she the first person to try to fly around the world?
"...she flew with copilot Lieutenant Commander Noonan"	I wonder how she picked him as her copilot.
"On July 2, the plane disappeared near Howland Island in the South Pacific."	How far is the South Pacific from Miami, where she began her flight attempt?

WRITING STRATEGY

Minilesson 87

Introducing Notetaking

Common Core State Standard: W.3.8

Objective: Understand various notetaking strategies.

Guiding Question: How can I keep track of researched facts?

Teach/Model

Read and discuss pp. 100–101. Explain that these pages show ways students recorded facts they found during research. Point out that the right-hand column of the log includes the student's questions and ideas about the facts.

Practice/Apply

Have students compare the notetaking strategies shown on these pages. Guide students to discuss the types of information included and the pros and cons of each strategy.

Minilesson 88

Citing Reference Sources

Common Core State Standard: W.3.8

Objective: Understand how to record information about sources.

Guiding Question: How can I remember where I found facts?

Teach/Model

Review the note cards on p. 100. Point out that the student wrote the source of the information on the bottom of each card. Explain that this allows the student to go back to the source at a later time.

Practice/Apply

Have students discuss the information included in the source citation. Guide them to recognize that different information is recorded for print and online materials.

Writing to a Prompt

Writing to a Prompt

A prompt is a writing assignment. Sometimes teachers give timed writing assignments for class exercises or tests.

Writing to a Prompt

- Read the prompt carefully.
- Note whether it asks you to give information, express opinions, or persuade someone.
- Plan your writing before you begin to draft.
- Restate the key parts of the prompt in your topic sentence.
- If you have a time limit, then plan your time carefully.

Prompt:
Think about how to take care of a plant. Now write a paragraph describing things a plant needs to grow.

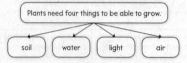

soil   water   light   air

Draft

Plants need four things to be able to grow. These four things are soil, light, water, and air. Plants get nutrients from the soil to help them grow. Also, they use light from the sun for energy. The plants cannot live on just light. They put the sunlight, water, and gases from the air together to make oxygen and sugar. The plants use the sugar to grow. We use the oxygen to breathe!

Prompts

Prompts often ask for different kinds of writing. Here is an example of a narrative prompt:

> Everyone has a favorite pastime. Think about how you like to spend your free time. Now write a story about a day you spent enjoying your favorite pastime.

Here are some other types of written prompts:

Fictional Narrative	Persuasive Writing
These prompts ask you to "tell a story."	These prompts ask you to "convince" or "persuade."
Informative Writing	**Response to Literature**
These prompts ask you to "tell or explain why."	These prompts ask you to answer questions about a piece you read.

Here is an example of a persuasive prompt:

> Many people have a favorite type of music. Think about the music you like. Now write a letter persuading a friend that the type of music you enjoy is the best.

WRITING STRATEGY

Minilesson 89

Writing to a Prompt

Common Core State Standard: W.3.4

Objective: Understand the steps for writing to a prompt.

Guiding Question: What should I do when writing to a prompt?

Teach/Model

Read and discuss pp. 102–103. Tell students that underlining the key words in a prompt can be helpful. Explain that the prompt will let students know what type of writing to complete. For example, the prompt on p. 102 tells writers to describe what plants need to grow.

Practice/Apply

Work with students to identify key words in the prompts on p. 103.

Minilesson 90

Budgeting Time When You Write

Common Core State Standard: W.3.5

Objective: Understand how to budget time.

Guiding Question: How much time should I spend on each writing stage when given a time limit?

Teach/Model

Review p. 102. Remind students that some writing assignments have a time limit and that students need to prewrite, draft, and revise during this time. Explain the importance of budgeting their time.

Practice/Apply

Have students read the example of a persuasive prompt on p. 103. Have them discuss how they might budget their time if given 45 minutes to respond to this prompt.

Checklists and Rubrics

EVALUATION

Checklists and Rubrics

A **rubric** is a chart that helps you when you write and revise. Score 6 tells you what to aim for in your writing.

	• Focus • Support	• Organization
Score **6**	My writing is focused and supported by facts or details.	My writing has an introduction and conclusion. Ideas are clearly organized.
Score **5**	My writing is mostly focused and supported by facts or details.	My writing has an introduction and a conclusion. Ideas are mostly organized.
Score **4**	My writing is mostly focused and supported by some facts or details.	My writing has an introduction and a conclusion. Most ideas are organized.
Score **3**	Some of my writing is focused and supported by some facts or details.	My writing has an introduction or a conclusion but might be missing one. Some ideas are organized.
Score **2**	My writing is not focused and is supported by few facts or details.	My writing might not have an introduction or a conclusion. Few ideas are organized.
Score **1**	My writing is not focused or supported by facts or details.	My writing is missing an introduction and a conclusion. Few or no ideas are organized.

• Word Choice • Voice	• Conventions • Sentence Fluency
Ideas are linked with words and phrases. Words are specific. My voice connects with the reader in a unique way.	My writing has no errors in spelling, grammar, capitalization, or punctuation. There are a variety of sentences.
Most ideas are linked with words and phrases. Words are specific. My voice connects with the reader.	My writing has few errors in spelling, grammar, capitalization, or punctuation. There is some variety of sentences.
Some ideas are linked with words and phrases. Some words are specific. My voice connects with the reader.	My writing has some errors in spelling, grammar, capitalization, or punctuation. There is some variety of sentences.
Some ideas are linked with words or phrases. Few words are specific. My voice may connect with the reader.	My writing has some errors in spelling, grammar, capitalization, or punctuation. There is little variety of sentences.
Ideas may be linked with words or phrases. Few words are specific. My voice may connect with the reader.	My writing has many errors in spelling, grammar, capitalization, or punctuation. There is little variety of sentences. Some sentences are incomplete.
Ideas may not be linked with words or phrases. No words are specific. My voice does not connect with the reader.	My writing has many errors in spelling, grammar, capitalization, or punctuation. There is no variety of sentences. Sentences are incomplete.

WRITING STRATEGY

Minilesson 91

Introducing Checklists and Rubrics

Common Core State Standard: W.3.5

Objective: Understand how to use a rubric to write.

Guiding Question: How can a rubric be useful when writing?

Teach/Model

Review pp. 104–105. Point out the column headings and explain that a score of 6 in each column represents very good writing. Tell students that looking at the characteristics that earn a high score can help writers set goals for what to include in their work.

Practice/Apply

Have students compare the characteristics of different scores and discuss why a score of 6 would be better than a score of 3.

Minilesson 92

Using a Rubric to Evaluate and Revise

Common Core State Standard: W.3.5

Objective: Understand how to use a rubric to revise writing.

Guiding Question: How can a rubric help me revise my writing?

Teach/Model

Review pp. 104–105. Point out that the top row states the characteristics of well-written work. Students can read what would earn a score of 6 for each trait and then evaluate and improve their own writing according to the statements.

Practice/Apply

Have students use the rubric to evaluate a piece of their own writing and make needed revisions.

Summary

Summary

A **summary** tells the reader about the plot and characters in a book or story.

Parts of a Summary

- An introduction that tells the reader the name of the book and its author
- Body paragraphs that describe the main events in the plot
- A conclusion that tells the end of the story

Introduction
Gives the main idea of the book

Body
Tells about the characters and plot

Stuart Little by E.B. White

The book *Stuart Little* by E.B. White is about a mouse named Stuart and his adventures in a really big city. Stuart gets into a lot of problems, but he has good friends who help him.

Stuart Little was born into a family of humans. However, Stuart is a mouse! At first, it was weird for the family to be living with a mouse. After a while, the whole family loved Stuart because he was so nice. The Littles quickly learned what a good son Stuart was. When Mrs. Little dropped her ring down the sink, Stuart helped her. Stuart was so small that he was able to go right down the drain to get the ring!

Stuart also lived with a cat named Snowball. While the whole family loved Stuart, Snowball did not like him. Snowball was jealous of Stuart and all the attention he got from the rest of the family.

Other Transitions
Second
After that
Soon
Meanwhile
Eventually
Finally
Later

Snowball started being mean to Stuart. One day, Snowball got Stuart trapped in the window.

Stuart had many more adventures and got into trouble a lot. He was very curious. Once, he got lost in Central Park and got swept out to sea. A bird named Margalo saved him. Margalo took Stuart back to his home. Then Stuart and Margalo became very good friends.

One day, Stuart learned that some of the neighborhood cats were planning to eat Margalo. Stuart told his friend, and Margalo decided to fly away for good. Stuart became really sad after that. He missed his good friend a lot.

Soon after, Stuart Little decided to go look for Margalo. Stuart got a toy car that ran on gas and headed north. The book ends with Stuart leaving to find his friend and have more exciting adventures.

Conclusion
Describes the end of the book

Note how the author of this piece:

- Introduced the book by telling its title, author, and main character.

  The book *Stuart Little* by E.B. White is about a mouse named Stuart and his adventures in a really big city.

- Told the events of the story in time order.

Minilesson 93

Understanding the Summary

Common Core State Standards: W.3.2a, W.3.2c

Objective: Understand how to use the information about summaries presented in this lesson.

Guiding Question: How can I use these pages to help me write a good summary?

Teach/Model

Have students read the definition and Parts of a Summary. Explain that a summary tells readers a few of the most important parts of a story's plot without retelling every detail. Point out the summary's introduction and conclusion, and then read pp. 106–107 with students.

Practice/Apply

Have students identify the characters and main events discussed in the summary.

Minilesson 94

Using Time Order

Common Core State Standard: W.3.2c

Objective: Use transitions to establish time order.

Guiding Question: How do I show that events in my summary are presented in time order?

Teach/Model

Explain that the writer retold the events in time order, as they appeared in the book. Transition words were included to indicate the order of the events. Point out the list of Other Transitions on p. 106, telling students that these are other words that may be used to show the order in which events happened.

Practice/Apply

Have students locate time-order transitions in the summary (ex: *At first, After a while, Soon after*).

Cause-and-Effect Essay

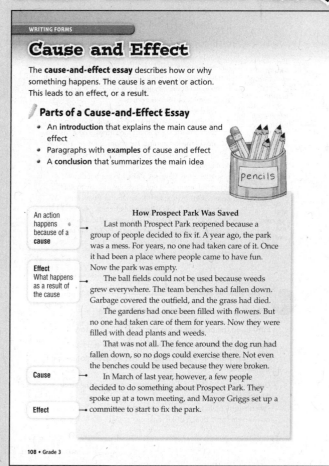

Cause and Effect

The **cause-and-effect essay** describes how or why something happens. The cause is an event or action. This leads to an effect, or a result.

Parts of a Cause-and-Effect Essay

- An **introduction** that explains the main cause and effect
- Paragraphs with **examples** of cause and effect
- A **conclusion** that summarizes the main idea

pencils

How Prospect Park Was Saved

An action happens because of a **cause**

Last month Prospect Park reopened because a group of people decided to fix it. A year ago, the park was a mess. For years, no one had taken care of it. Once it had been a place where people came to have fun. Now the park was empty.

Effect What happens as a result of the cause

The ball fields could not be used because weeds grew everywhere. The team benches had fallen down. Garbage covered the outfield, and the grass had died.

The gardens had once been filled with flowers. But no one had taken care of them for years. Now they were filled with dead plants and weeds.

That was not all. The fence around the dog run had fallen down, so no dogs could exercise there. Not even the benches could be used because they were broken.

Cause

In March of last year, however, a few people decided to do something about Prospect Park. They spoke up at a town meeting, and Mayor Griggs set up a

Effect

committee to start to fix the park.

These paragraphs offer more examples of cause and effect.

One group of people raised money. They convinced hardware stores to give materials for building, and many people gave money, too.

Another group got volunteers to work at the park each weekend. Soon the ball fields were better than ever. People made new gardens, benches, and even barbecue pits!

Finally, dog owners volunteered time to build a new dog run. They fixed fences and gates and put in water bowls. Soon it was a place that dogs would love.

The committee worked long and hard for almost a year. In the end, their work paid off. Last month, over a thousand people came to the park's grand re-opening.

Since then, the action in the park has not stopped. Little league and adult baseball teams play every day. Volunteers keep the gardens beautiful. The lawns are covered with soft, wonderful-smelling grass. Best of all, the dogs play whenever they want in the new dog run.

Conclusion

All this happened because a few people cared about making Prospect Park a great place for everyone.

Note how the writer of this piece:

- Began the essay by stating the main cause and effect. Another way the writer could have introduced the essay is to ask a question:
  How did people save Prospect Park?
- Went on to describe a situation.
- Continued by telling what was done to change that situation.
- Used a conclusion that summed up what was done.

Minilesson 95

Understanding the Cause-and-Effect Essay

Common Core State Standards: W.3.2a, W.3.2b

Objective: Understand how to use the information about cause-and-effect essays presented in this lesson.

Guiding Question: How can these pages help me write a good cause-and-effect essay?

Teach/Model

Read and discuss the definition, information, and essay on pp. 108–109. Explain that cause and effect relationships can be simplified using the word *so* (ex: … *so no dogs could exercise there*).

Practice/Apply

Have students identify other cause and effect relationships in the student model.

Minilesson 96

Writing a Conclusion

Common Core State Standard: W.3.2d

Objective: Write a conclusion to summarize the main idea.
Guiding Question: How do I write an ending to my essay?

Teach/Model

Explain that a conclusion wraps up the essay by restating the main idea. This reminds readers of the main point and creates a sense that the essay is complete.

Practice/Apply

Have students identify both the main idea of the essay and the conclusion that reviews this idea. Ask students to suggest other ways to summarize the main idea and create an effective conclusion for the essay.

Problem-Solution Essay

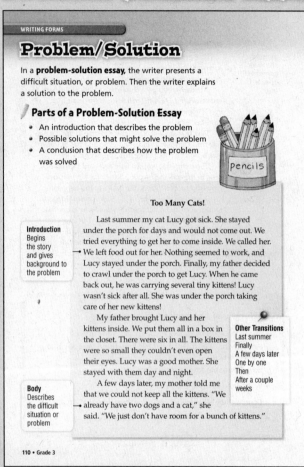

Problem/Solution

In a **problem-solution essay**, the writer presents a difficult situation, or problem. Then the writer explains a solution to the problem.

Parts of a Problem-Solution Essay

- An introduction that describes the problem
- Possible solutions that might solve the problem
- A conclusion that describes how the problem was solved

Too Many Cats!

Introduction
Begins the story and gives background to the problem

Last summer my cat Lucy got sick. She stayed under the porch for days and would not come out. We tried everything to get her to come inside. We called her. We left food out for her. Nothing seemed to work, and Lucy stayed under the porch. Finally, my father decided to crawl under the porch to get Lucy. When he came back out, he was carrying several tiny kittens! Lucy wasn't sick after all. She was under the porch taking care of her new kittens!

My father brought Lucy and her kittens inside. We put them all in a box in the closet. There were six in all. The kittens were so small they couldn't even open their eyes. Lucy was a good mother. She stayed with them day and night.

Other Transitions
Last summer
Finally
A few days later
One by one
Then
After a couple weeks

Body
Describes the difficult situation or problem

A few days later, my mother told me that we could not keep all the kittens. "We already have two dogs and a cat," she said. "We just don't have room for a bunch of kittens."

110 • Grade 3

This paragraph explores ways to solve the problem.

Here the author describes her solution to the problem.

I was sad, but I knew she was right. Caring for six kittens is a lot of work. My mother asked me what I wanted to do about the kittens. We could bring them all down to the animal shelter. Or we could try to find good homes for them ourselves.

We decided to find homes for the kittens. That way we could make sure each kitten found a good family to live with. I made signs about the kittens. The signs had pictures of the kittens and our phone number. Then we put up the signs in places like the grocery store and the post office.

Conclusion
Describes what happened when she tried her solution

After a few days, we started to get phone calls about the kittens. Different people came by to see the kittens. One by one each kitten found a new home. We made sure each kitten was going to nice people. Finally, there was one kitten left. He was small and quiet. After a couple of weeks, no one came to look at the last kitten. Then one day my father said to me, "Let's keep this one." I was so happy! We got a new kitten!

Note how the author of this piece:

- Introduced the problem to the reader by telling a story.

- Used transition words and phrases to move the story along.
  A few days later, my mother told me that we could not keep all the kittens.

- Used dialogue to describe the problem and make the story sound realistic.
  "We already have two dogs and a cat," she said. "We just don't have room for a bunch of kittens."

Problem/Solution • 111

WRITING MODELS AND FORMS

Minilesson 97

Understanding the Problem-Solution Essay

Common Core State Standards: W.3.2a, W.3.2d

Objective: Understand the characteristics of a good problem-solution essay.

Guiding Question: What should I include in a problem-solution essay?

Teach/Model

Read the definition, bulleted list, and sample essay on pp. 110–111. Explain that an essay may discuss more than one possible way to solve the problem.

Practice/Apply

Have students identify the problem and the possible solutions that the writer discussed.

Minilesson 98

Using Dialogue

Common Core State Standard: W.3.3b

Objective: Use dialogue to make an essay sound realistic.

Guiding Question: What can I add to make my essay more interesting and realistic?

Teach/Model

Remind students that dialogue refers to the words spoken by the characters. Explain that dialogue can make the writing more realistic and more interesting for readers. Restate the final paragraph on p. 110 without dialogue. Then reread the dialogue to show how it enhances the essay.

Practice/Apply

Have students locate dialogue in the essay and discuss other places the writer could have added it.

Writing for Science and Math

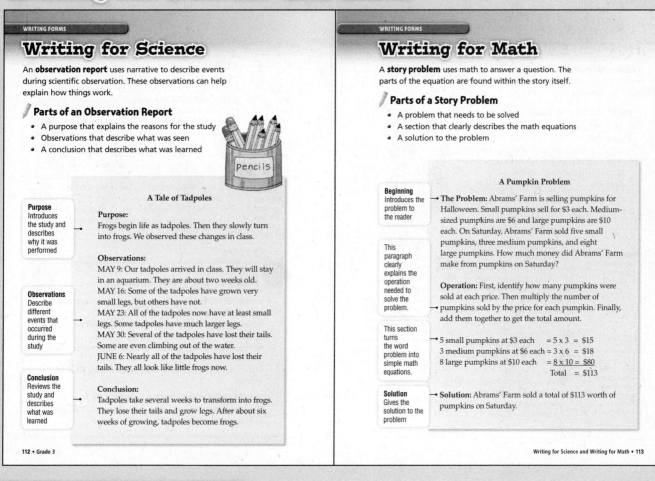

Writing for Science

An **observation report** uses narrative to describe events during scientific observation. These observations can help explain how things work.

Parts of an Observation Report

- A purpose that explains the reasons for the study
- Observations that describe what was seen
- A conclusion that describes what was learned

A Tale of Tadpoles

Purpose
Introduces the study and describes why it was performed

Purpose:
Frogs begin life as tadpoles. Then they slowly turn into frogs. We observed these changes in class.

Observations:
MAY 9: Our tadpoles arrived in class. They will stay in an aquarium. They are about two weeks old.
MAY 16: Some of the tadpoles have grown very small legs, but others have not.
MAY 23: All of the tadpoles now have at least small legs. Some tadpoles have much larger legs.
MAY 30: Several of the tadpoles have lost their tails. Some are even climbing out of the water.
JUNE 6: Nearly all of the tadpoles have lost their tails. They all look like little frogs now.

Observations
Describe different events that occurred during the study

Conclusion
Reviews the study and describes what was learned

Conclusion:
Tadpoles take several weeks to transform into frogs. They lose their tails and grow legs. After about six weeks of growing, tadpoles become frogs.

Writing for Math

A **story problem** uses math to answer a question. The parts of the equation are found within the story itself.

Parts of a Story Problem

- A problem that needs to be solved
- A section that clearly describes the math equations
- A solution to the problem

A Pumpkin Problem

Beginning
Introduces the problem to the reader

The Problem: Abrams' Farm is selling pumpkins for Halloween. Small pumpkins sell for $3 each. Medium-sized pumpkins are $6 and large pumpkins are $10 each. On Saturday, Abrams' Farm sold five small pumpkins, three medium pumpkins, and eight large pumpkins. How much money did Abrams' Farm make from pumpkins on Saturday?

This paragraph clearly explains the operation needed to solve the problem.

Operation: First, identify how many pumpkins were sold at each price. Then multiply the number of pumpkins sold by the price for each pumpkin. Finally, add them together to get the total amount.

This section turns the word problem into simple math equations.

5 small pumpkins at $3 each $= 5 \times 3 = \$15$
3 medium pumpkins at $6 each $= 3 \times 6 = \$18$
8 large pumpkins at $10 each $= \underline{8 \times 10 = \$80}$
Total $= \$113$

Solution
Gives the solution to the problem

Solution: Abrams' Farm sold a total of $113 worth of pumpkins on Saturday.

WRITING MODELS AND FORMS

Minilesson 99

Understanding the Observation Report

Common Core State Standards: W.3.2a, W.3.2d

Objective: Understand what belongs in an observation report.

Guiding Question: What should I include when I write for science?

Teach/Model

Read and discuss p. 112. Point out that each observation begins with a date, followed by a detailed description of what the writer observed. Add that the observations are related to the purpose of the study.

Practice/Apply

Have students discuss how each observation relates to the purpose of the study (ex: *They show how the tadpoles are changing as they turn into frogs*).

Minilesson 100

Understanding the Parts of a Story Problem

Common Core State Standards: W.3.2a, W.3.2d

Objective: Understand what to include in a story problem.

Guiding Question: What do I need to include when I write to solve a math story problem?

Teach/Model

Read and discuss p. 113. Explain that many story problems require students to follow sequential steps in order to solve the problem. Transition words such as *first, then,* and *finally* help show the correct order.

Practice/Apply

Direct students to the "Problem" section and have them identify the facts in the word problem. Discuss how the writer turned the facts into equations to solve the problem.

How-to Essay

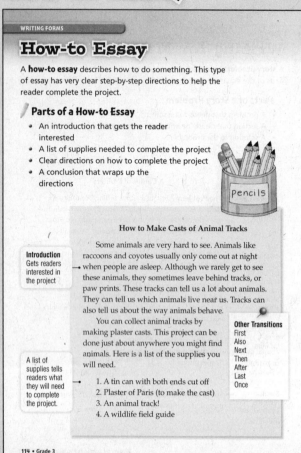

How-to Essay

A **how-to essay** describes how to do something. This type of essay has very clear step-by-step directions to help the reader complete the project.

Parts of a How-to Essay

- An introduction that gets the reader interested
- A list of supplies needed to complete the project
- Clear directions on how to complete the project
- A conclusion that wraps up the directions

How to Make Casts of Animal Tracks

Introduction — Gets readers interested in the project

Some animals are very hard to see. Animals like raccoons and coyotes usually only come out at night when people are asleep. Although we rarely get to see these animals, they sometimes leave behind tracks, or paw prints. These tracks can tell us a lot about animals. They can tell us which animals live near us. Tracks can also tell us about the way animals behave.

You can collect animal tracks by making plaster casts. This project can be done just about anywhere you might find animals. Here is a list of the supplies you will need.

Other Transitions
First
Also
Next
Then
After
Last
Once

A list of supplies tells readers what they will need to complete the project.

1. A tin can with both ends cut off
2. Plaster of Paris (to make the cast)
3. An animal track!
4. A wildlife field guide

114 • Grade 3

Body — Guides readers through the project step by step

First, locate an animal track in your backyard or on a hiking trail. This track should have obvious parts, such as toes, claws, and a footpad.

Next, remove any debris from the track, such as leaves or sticks. Then place the tin can around the track. Press the can into the soil about 1-inch deep.

After you press the can into the soil, stir ½ cup of Plaster of Paris with water until the mixture is thick like pancake batter. Pour the mixture into the can and cover the track. There should be about 1 inch of plaster in the bottom of the can. Let the plaster dry for at least one hour before removing the can from the ground. Then let the plaster cast dry for another 24 hours before removing it from the can.

Conclusion — Tells readers what they can do after they have completed the project

Once you remove the cast, use your field guide to help you identify what animal made the track.

Note how the author of this piece:

- Introduced the project by getting the reader interested in the subject.
  Other ways she could have introduced the project are to ask a question or state a fact.
  Have you ever wanted to learn about animals that are hard to see?
  Scientists use animal tracks to learn about many kinds of animals.
- Told the reader what to do after completing the project.
  Once you remove the cast from the can, use your field guide to help you identify what animal made the track.

How-to Essay • 115

WRITING MODELS AND FORMS

Minilesson 101

Understanding the How-to Essay

Common Core State Standards: W.3.2a, W.3.2c

Objective: Understand how to use the information about a how-to essay presented in this lesson.

Guiding Question: How can I use these pages to help me write a how-to essay?

Teach/Model

Read and discuss pp. 114–115. Explain that the order of the steps in a how-to essay is important. Rather than numbering the steps, transitions are used to show sequence. Discuss the list of Other Transitions.

Practice/Apply

Have students identify the order of the steps and find the transition words used in the essay.

Minilesson 102

Writing an Introduction

Common Core State Standard: W.3.2a

Objective: Understand how to write a strong introduction.

Guiding Question: How can I introduce a project in a way that interests the readers?

Teach/Model

Discuss how the introduction on p. 114 makes finding tracks and learning about animals sound exciting. Explain that the introduction to a how-to essay should get readers interested in reading more about a project.

Practice/Apply

Have students suggest a question, fact, or exclamation to introduce the project. Discuss interesting ways to introduce other projects (ex: building a birdhouse, baking a cake, etc.).

Explanation

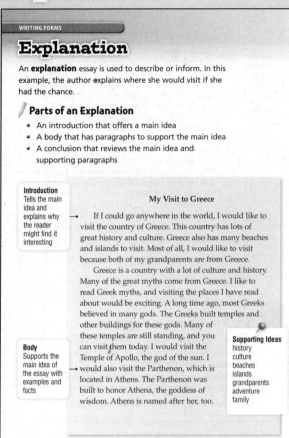

WRITING FORMS

Explanation

An **explanation** essay is used to describe or inform. In this example, the author explains where she would visit if she had the chance.

Parts of an Explanation

- An introduction that offers a main idea
- A body that has paragraphs to support the main idea
- A conclusion that reviews the main idea and supporting paragraphs

Introduction
Tells the main idea and explains why the reader might find it interesting

My Visit to Greece

If I could go anywhere in the world, I would like to visit the country of Greece. This country has lots of great history and culture. Greece also has many beaches and islands to visit. Most of all, I would like to visit because both of my grandparents are from Greece.

Greece is a country with a lot of culture and history. Many of the great myths come from Greece. I like to read Greek myths, and visiting the places I have read about would be exciting. A long time ago, most Greeks believed in many gods. The Greeks built temples and other buildings for these gods. Many of these temples are still standing, and you can visit them today. I would visit the Temple of Apollo, the god of the sun. I would also visit the Parthenon, which is located in Athens. The Parthenon was built to honor Athena, the goddess of wisdom. Athens is named after her, too.

Body
Supports the main idea of the essay with examples and facts

Supporting Ideas
history
culture
beaches
islands
grandparents
adventure
family

116 • Grade 3

Each supporting paragraph has a topic sentence that explains the main idea of the paragraph.

Greece is located on the Mediterranean Sea, so the weather is terrific all year round. One of my favorite parts of Greece would be visiting the beaches and the many small villages around the countryside.

Most of all, I would like to visit Greece because my grandmother and grandfather are from there. Both of my grandparents were born in Athens in 1940. They got married in 1960 and then moved to the United States. They have gone back to visit friends and family many times. My parents have gone with them, too. When they got back home last time they told me a lot of funny stories about our family in Greece. I would really like to meet my Greek cousins. My grandmother says I can go with them to Greece next summer. I can't wait!

Conclusion
Reviews the main ideas of the essay and explains why the subject is interesting

Greece is a country full of history. The country has done a terrific job preserving this history for the world to come see. My own family history is part of Greece, too. Because of this, Greece is the one place in the world I would like to visit.

Note how the author of this piece:

- Used the first paragraph to introduce the main idea and supporting details.
- Included topic sentences that introduced the main idea of each paragraph.
  Most of all I would like to visit Greece because my grandmother and grandfather are from there.
- Reviewed the main idea and supporting details in the conclusion.

Explanation • 117

Minilesson 103

Understanding the Explanation

Common Core State Standards: W.3.2a, W.3.2d

Objective: Use the pages to understand an explanation.
Guiding Question: What are the important parts of an explanation?

Teach/Model

Read the definition, bulleted list, and model on pp. 116–117. Point out the main idea of the essay and explain that each paragraph has a main idea of its own. These support the main idea of the entire essay. Details in each paragraph support those main ideas.

Practice/Apply

Have students read the list of supporting ideas on p. 116. Then find the ideas in the essay. Discuss how each supports the main idea of its paragraph.

Minilesson 104

Using Supporting Details

Common Core State Standards: W.3.2a, W.3.2b

Objective: Recognize types of supporting details.
Guiding Question: What can I use to support the main idea?

Teach/Model

Explain that supporting ideas help to explain the main idea of the essay. Facts, examples, definitions, and personal anecdotes can be used as supporting details. Writers select details that best support the main idea and that also fit the audience and purpose of the piece.

Practice/Apply

Have students find examples of historical facts, personal anecdotes, and definitions in the sample essay. Discuss how these help explain the main idea and make the essay interesting.

Research Report

Research Report

In a **research report**, the author informs the reader about a topic. The author first researches the topic and then uses these facts to create an essay.

Parts of a Research Report

- An introduction that tells the reader something interesting about the topic
- A body that gives details and facts to support the main idea
- A conclusion that reviews the main ideas about the topic

Introduction
Tells about the subject and explains why the author finds it interesting

Salamanders!

Salamanders are very interesting animals. They come in all different sizes and colors and can be found just about anywhere. You can even find salamanders in your backyard!

Salamanders have a fascinating lifecycle. Like frogs, salamanders are amphibians. Some salamanders lay their eggs in lakes or ponds. When the eggs hatch, the little salamanders have gills to help them breathe under water. Over a few weeks, salamanders grow and change. They lose their gills and breathe air. Then they leave the pond and walk on land. Adult salamanders live under rotten logs, leaves, or rocks in wet areas.

Body
Has paragraphs that support the author's main ideas

Many salamanders in North America do not have lungs. These salamanders can breathe right through their skin! Because of this, salamanders have to keep their skin moist. This is why salamanders like to live in wet or muddy places. If you ever catch a salamander, make sure your hands are wet. Handling a salamander with dry hands can hurt their wet skin.

These paragraphs continue to support the author's main idea. They also offer many interesting facts about salamanders.

There are almost 500 different species of salamanders found around the world. About 100 different kinds of salamanders live in the United States. The Great Smoky Mountains National Park is known as the "Salamander Capital of the World." This is because so many different kinds of salamanders live in the park.

The largest salamander in the United States is called the hellbender. It can grow up to two feet long! These salamanders are very hard to find because they only come out at night. Also, hellbenders live in large rivers and spend most of their time hiding under rocks. The hellbender is big, but it is not the largest salamander in the world. The Chinese giant salamander can grow as large as six feet long! Luckily these giant creatures are only found in Asia.

Conclusion
Reviews the main idea and supporting paragraphs

Salamanders are very cool animals. There are many different kinds of salamanders, too. These animals can be found just about anywhere. Next time you are out hiking, turn over some rotten logs. You'll never know what you might find hiding there!

Note how the writer of this piece:

- Introduced the topic of the essay in the first paragraph. Another way the writer could have introduced the topic is to ask a question to grab the reader's attention. Which animal can be many shapes and sizes and live in your own backyard? Salamanders are very interesting animals.
- Included supporting paragraphs with interesting facts

Minilesson 105

Understanding the Research Report

Common Core State Standards: W.3.2a, W.3.2d

Objective: Use the pages to understand a research report.

Guiding Question: What should be included when I write to inform about a topic?

Teach/Model

Read the information and model on pp. 118–119. Point out the introduction, the supporting ideas in the body, and the conclusion. Note that the body of research reports is organized with similar information grouped together.

Practice/Apply

Have students identify sets of similar information grouped together in the model.

Minilesson 106

Writing Topic Sentences

Common Core State Standard: W.3.2a

Objective: Understand the purpose of a topic sentence.

Guiding Question: How can I tell what a paragraph is about?

Teach/Model

Explain that each paragraph of a research report has a topic sentence that tells what information will be included in that paragraph. That topic sentence gives the main idea of the paragraph and is usually the first sentence.

Practice/Apply

Have students identify the topic sentence of each paragraph and the details and information that support it.

Graphs, Diagrams, and Charts

WRITING FORMS

Graphs, Diagrams, and Charts

Graphs, diagrams, and charts help make ideas clear. You can use them in your informative writing, such as a research report.

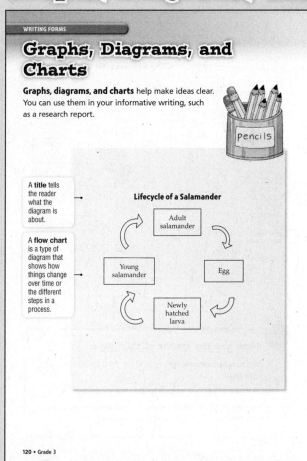

A **title** tells the reader what the diagram is about.

A **flow chart** is a type of diagram that shows how things change over time or the different steps in a process.

Lifecycle of a Salamander

Adult salamander → Egg → Newly hatched larva → Young salamander → (Adult salamander)

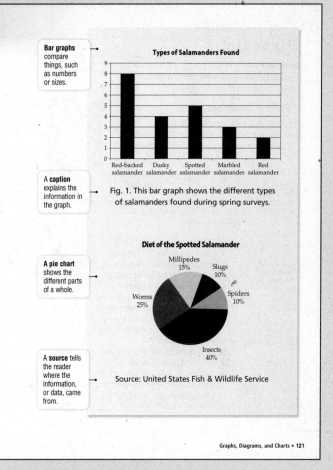

Bar graphs compare things, such as numbers or sizes.

Types of Salamanders Found

Red-backed salamander: 8
Dusky salamander: 4
Spotted salamander: 5
Marbled salamander: 3
Red salamander: 2

A **caption** explains the information in the graph.

Fig. 1. This bar graph shows the different types of salamanders found during spring surveys.

A **pie chart** shows the different parts of a whole.

Diet of the Spotted Salamander

Millipedes 15%
Slugs 10%
Spiders 10%
Insects 40%
Worms 25%

A **source** tells the reader where the information, or data, came from.

Source: United States Fish & Wildlife Service

WRITING MODELS AND FORMS

Minilesson 107

Understanding Graphs, Diagrams, and Charts

Common Core State Standard: W.3.2a

Objective: Understand types of visual aids.

Guiding Question: How can I show data to my readers?

Teach/Model

Read and discuss pp. 120–121. Explain that visual aids such as these can present and organize information in a way that makes information clear to readers. Add that line graphs, tables, and picture graphs are also used to display data.

Practice/Apply

Have students identify the purpose of each visual aid. Discuss the types of information that might be shown by each kind.

Minilesson 108

Using a Pie Chart

Common Core State Standard: W.3.2a

Objective: Understand how data is presented in a pie chart.

Guiding Question: What is shown by a pie chart?

Teach/Model

Point out the pie chart on p. 121 and tell students that pie charts are also called *circle graphs*. Explain that each section of the graph represents a percent of the whole and that the sum of the sections is 100%. Point out that, with a quick glance, readers can see that the largest section is *insects*, so they can tell that insects are the largest part of the diet of most salamanders.

Practice/Apply

Have students give examples of when they might include pie charts in their writing.

Directions

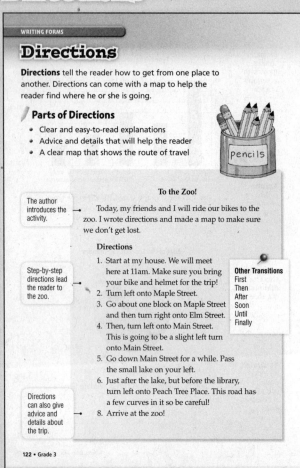

Directions

Directions tell the reader how to get from one place to another. Directions can come with a map to help the reader find where he or she is going.

Parts of Directions

- Clear and easy-to-read explanations
- Advice and details that will help the reader
- A clear map that shows the route of travel

To the Zoo!

The author introduces the activity.

Today, my friends and I will ride our bikes to the zoo. I wrote directions and made a map to make sure we don't get lost.

Directions

Step-by-step directions lead the reader to the zoo.

1. Start at my house. We will meet here at 11am. Make sure you bring your bike and helmet for the trip!
2. Turn left onto Maple Street.
3. Go about one block on Maple Street and then turn right onto Elm Street.
4. Then, turn left onto Main Street. This is going to be a slight left turn onto Main Street.
5. Go down Main Street for a while. Pass the small lake on your left.
6. Just after the lake, but before the library, turn left onto Peach Tree Place. This road has a few curves in it so be careful!
8. Arrive at the zoo!

Other Transitions
First
Then
After
Soon
Until
Finally

Directions can also give advice and details about the trip.

122 • Grade 3

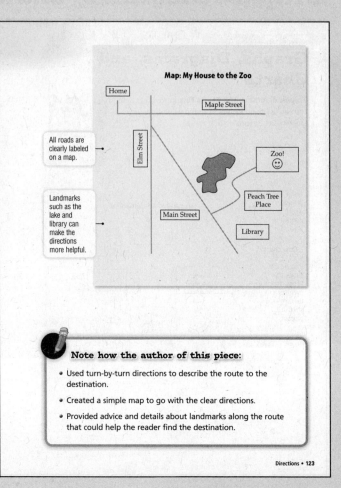

All roads are clearly labeled on a map.

Landmarks such as the lake and library can make the directions more helpful.

Note how the author of this piece:

- Used turn-by-turn directions to describe the route to the destination.
- Created a simple map to go with the clear directions.
- Provided advice and details about landmarks along the route that could help the reader find the destination.

Directions • 123

WRITING MODELS AND FORMS

Minilesson 109

Understanding Directions

Common Core State Standard: W.3.4

Objective: Understand how to write complete directions.
Guiding Question: What should I include when giving instructions for how to get somewhere?

Teach/Model

Read p. 122 together. Explain that exact words and details help readers understand and follow the directions. Point out that the writer also included advice to help readers make the trip.

Practice/Apply

Have students identify examples of exact words and details *(street names, "slight left turn," landmarks)* and advice *(bring your helmet, be careful)*. Discuss why these might help readers.

Minilesson 110

Using a Map

Common Core State Standard: W.3.2a

Objective: Understand how a map is helpful.
Guiding Question: What should my map show?

Teach/Model

Read p. 123. Explain that the map shows what is discussed in the directions on p. 122. Point out street names, landmarks, the beginning point, and the end point. Tell students that the writer included landmarks that the reader could easily recognize.

Practice/Apply

Have pairs work together. Instruct one student to read the directions aloud as the other follows along on the map.

Friendly Letter/Thank-You Letter

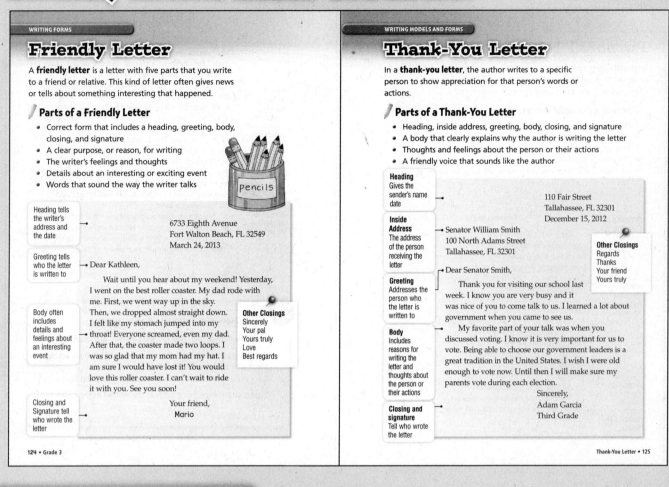

Friendly Letter

A **friendly letter** is a letter with five parts that you write to a friend or relative. This kind of letter often gives news or tells about something interesting that happened.

Parts of a Friendly Letter

- Correct form that includes a heading, greeting, body, closing, and signature
- A clear purpose, or reason, for writing
- The writer's feelings and thoughts
- Details about an interesting or exciting event
- Words that sound the way the writer talks

Heading tells the writer's address and the date

6733 Eighth Avenue
Fort Walton Beach, FL 32549
March 24, 2013

Greeting tells who the letter is written to

Dear Kathleen,

    Wait until you hear about my weekend! Yesterday, I went on the best roller coaster. My dad rode with me. First, we went way up in the sky. Then, we dropped almost straight down. I felt like my stomach jumped into my throat! Everyone screamed, even my dad. After that, the coaster made two loops. I was so glad that my mom had my hat. I am sure I would have lost it! You would love this roller coaster. I can't wait to ride it with you. See you soon!

Body often includes details and feelings about an interesting event

Other Closings
Sincerely
Your pal
Yours truly
Love
Best regards

Your friend,
Mario

Closing and Signature tell who wrote the letter

124 • Grade 3

Thank-You Letter

In a **thank-you letter**, the author writes to a specific person to show appreciation for that person's words or actions.

Parts of a Thank-You Letter

- Heading, inside address, greeting, body, closing, and signature
- A body that clearly explains why the author is writing the letter
- Thoughts and feelings about the person or their actions
- A friendly voice that sounds like the author

Heading
Gives the sender's name date

110 Fair Street
Tallahassee, FL 32301
December 15, 2012

Inside Address
The address of the person receiving the letter

Senator William Smith
100 North Adams Street
Tallahassee, FL 32301

Other Closings
Regards
Thanks
Your friend
Yours truly

Greeting
Addresses the person who the letter is written to

Dear Senator Smith,

    Thank you for visiting our school last week. I know you are very busy and it was nice of you to come talk to us. I learned a lot about government when you came to see us.

Body
Includes reasons for writing the letter and thoughts about the person or their actions

    My favorite part of your talk was when you discussed voting. I know it is very important for us to vote. Being able to choose our government leaders is a great tradition in the United States. I wish I were old enough to vote now. Until then I will make sure my parents vote during each election.

Sincerely,
Adam Garcia
Third Grade

Closing and signature
Tell who wrote the letter

Thank-You Letter • 125

WRITING MODELS AND FORMS

Minilesson 111

Understanding Friendly Letters

Common Core State Standard: W.3.4

Objective: Use the page to understand friendly letters.

Guiding Question: How do I write a letter to someone I know?

Teach/Model

Read and discuss p. 124. Explain that this is a letter that the writer sent to a friend; it uses informal language and shares ideas and events that would interest the reader. Point out the commas following the greeting and closing. Add that the closing and signature are aligned to the right and that the body paragraph is indented.

Practice/Apply

Have students identify the five parts of friendly letters and suggest other content to include in them.

Minilesson 112

Understanding Thank-You Letters

Common Core State Standard: W.3.4

Objective: Use the page to understand thank-you letters.

Guiding Question: What should be included when I write to thank someone?

Teach/Model

Read and discuss p. 125. Point out that a formal thank-you letter includes six parts as well as an explanation of what the writer is thankful for and why.

Practice/Apply

Have students identify differences between a friendly letter and a formal thank-you letter (ex: in a formal letter, heading includes receiver's address; signature adds identifying information; language is more formal; closing is more formal).

Personal Narrative

Personal Narrative

A **personal narrative** is a true story about an interesting or important event in the writer's life. A personal narrative about a writer's life may also be called an autobiography.

Parts of a Personal Narrative

- A beginning that pulls readers into the story
- Real events told in the order that they happened
- Interesting details about the people and events in the story
- A first-person point of view
- An ending that wraps up the story or tells how the writer felt

Beginning
Grabs the readers' attention

Middle
Tells what happened in time order

Interesting details describe sights, sounds, and feelings.

Learning to Fly

I will never forget the day I learned to fly. I didn't have wings, though, and I didn't use an airplane. All I had was a special jacket called a harness to keep me from falling to the ground. The activity is called zip-lining. I tried it for the first time when my family went on vacation to Montana.

At first I was scared to go zip-lining. My instructor, George, said that I would walk up a trail to a wooden deck. The deck was on the edge of a cliff 70 feet high! Then George would attach my harness to a long steel line. The line ran 200 feet across and ended at another deck below. Finally, I would jump off the top deck and zip through the air to the lower deck.

Walking up to the deck was the easy part. I liked looking up at all the tall trees

Other Transitions
First
Next
After that
During
After a while
Meanwhile
Later
Last

and hearing the birds sing. But as soon as we got to the deck, I became dizzy. My heart started to pound. I told George that I didn't think I could do it.

George patted me on the back and smiled. He said lots of people are scared at first. He explained how safe it was to go zip-lining. He said I looked very brave.

When I was ready, George attached my harness to the zip line. He reminded me to hold the rope that held my harness to the line. I took a deep breath and closed my eyes. Then I stepped off the deck.

Whoosh! The air whipped across my face and through my hair. I opened my eyes and saw the ground speed by below me. I was flying! George was right. Zip-lining was a lot of fun! It was even better than riding a roller coaster.

My parents were waiting for me when I got to the lower deck. I gave them a big smile and a hug. Then I told them that I couldn't wait to go zip-lining again. After all, nothing is more exciting than flying!

These paragraphs tell more about what happened and how the writer felt.

Ending
Tells how the story worked out and how the writer felt

Note how the author of this piece:

- Wrote an introduction that grabbed readers' attention.
- Other ways she could have introduced the story include asking the reader a question or jumping into the action.

Have you ever watched a bird and wished you could fly?

I gripped the rope on my harness and stared at the ground below.

126 • Grade 3

Personal Narrative • 127

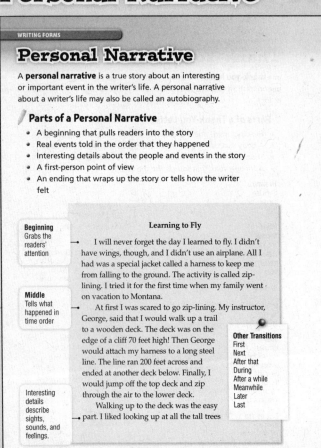

WRITING MODELS AND FORMS

Minilesson 113

Understanding the Personal Narrative

Common Core State Standards: W.3.3b, W.3.3d

Objective: Understand the parts of a personal narrative.
Guiding Question: What belongs in a story about me?

Teach/Model

Read pp. 126–127. Discuss the organization and what should be part of each section. Explain that a first-person point of view means that the story is told by someone who is part of the story and uses words such as *I*, *me*, and *my*. In a third-person point of view, the story is told by an outside narrator.

Practice/Apply

Have students discuss how the first-person point of view got their attention and kept them interested in the story.

Minilesson 114

Using Details That Describe

Common Core State Standard: W.3.3b

Objective: Recognize interesting sensory details.
Guiding Question: How can I involve the readers' senses?

Teach/Model

Explain that good writers include interesting details to help audiences involve their senses. Point out the last box on p. 126, explaining that these details describe sights, sounds, and feelings. Add that narratives may also include details about smell or taste.

Practice/Apply

Have students identify details in the student model that describe sights, sounds, and feelings. Discuss how these details make the story more interesting.

Biography

Biography

A **biography** is a true story about a person's life. It tells why that person is special or interesting.

Parts of a Biography

- A beginning, middle, and end
- Interesting facts and details about the person
- Events told in time order

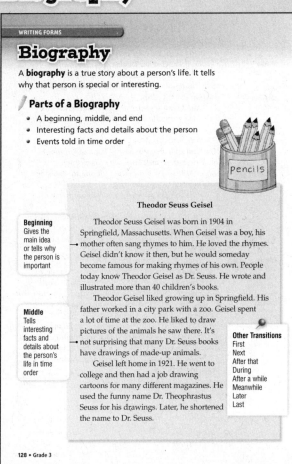

Theodor Seuss Geisel

Beginning
Gives the main idea or tells why the person is important

Theodor Seuss Geisel was born in 1904 in Springfield, Massachusetts. When Geisel was a boy, his mother often sang rhymes to him. He loved the rhymes. Geisel didn't know it then, but he would someday become famous for making rhymes of his own. People today know Theodor Geisel as Dr. Seuss. He wrote and illustrated more than 40 children's books.

Middle
Tells interesting facts and details about the person's life in time order

Theodor Geisel liked growing up in Springfield. His father worked in a city park with a zoo. Geisel spent a lot of time at the zoo. He liked to draw pictures of the animals he saw there. It's not surprising that many Dr. Seuss books have drawings of made-up animals.

Geisel left home in 1921. He went to college and then had a job drawing cartoons for many different magazines. He used the funny name Dr. Theophrastus Seuss for his drawings. Later, he shortened the name to Dr. Seuss.

Other Transitions
First
Next
After that
During
After a while
Meanwhile
Later
Last

In 1937, "Dr. Seuss" published his first children's book, *And to Think That I Saw It on Mulberry Street*. At first, publishers didn't like his book. Geisel had to send it to 27 different publishers before one of them accepted it! But readers loved Dr. Seuss's rhymes and cartoons. He published 10 more books between 1938 and 1956.

Geisel had a big challenge in 1957. His publisher asked him to write a book with only 225 different words. The words had to be ones that students in first grade could read on their own. Theodor wrote *The Cat in the Hat*. It became one of his most popular books. Three years later, he published *Green Eggs and Ham*. This book had only 50 different words.

End
Wraps up the biography and gives a final thought

Theodor Seuss Geisel died in 1991. His books have sold over 200 million copies. They also have been printed in 20 different languages. He was one of the world's greatest children's authors.

Note how the author of this piece:

- Wrapped up this piece by giving a final thought.

  Other ways to conclude a biography include: explaining how the person's work is still being used today or telling how the person made a difference.

  Theodor Geisel's books are still being read in homes and classrooms today.

  Theodor Geisel made a difference in the lives of children around the world. He made reading fun.

WRITING MODELS AND FORMS

Minilesson 115

Understanding the Biography

Common Core State Standards: W.3.2a, W.3.2b

Objective: Understand how to write a biography.

Guiding Question: How do I tell about a person's life?

Teach/Model

Read and discuss the information and model on pp. 128–129. Point out that the student writer used dates to help establish time order in the biography. Explain that dates are more specific than other time-order transitions and that dates help readers understand exactly when events occurred.

Practice/Apply

Have students locate dates and time-order words in the model. Ask them where other dates could have been added.

Minilesson 116

Choosing Facts for a Biography

Common Core State Standard: W.3.2b

Objective: Recognize which facts to include in a biography.

Guiding Question: What types of information should I tell about someone?

Teach/Model

Review the model on pp. 128–129. Point out that the biography tells about Dr. Seuss's life from childhood through adulthood. Explain that since Dr. Seuss is famous for being an artist and writer, most facts in the biography focus on these areas of his life. The details help readers understand how he developed his career.

Practice/Apply

Have students explain how the facts in each paragraph relate to Dr. Seuss's writing and drawing.

Fictional Narrative

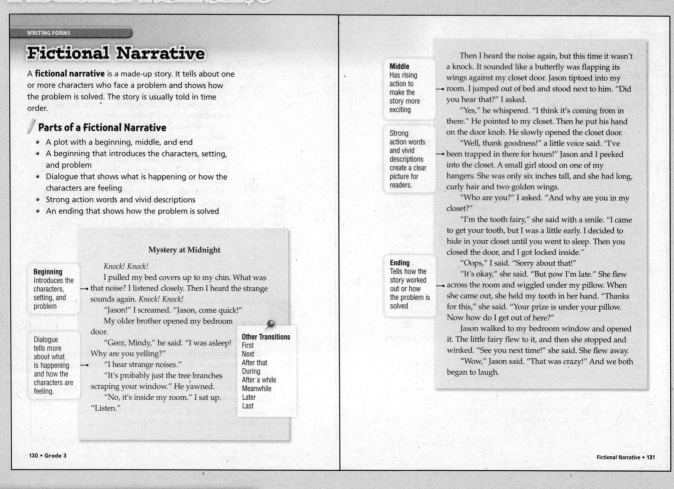

Fictional Narrative

A **fictional narrative** is a made-up story. It tells about one or more characters who face a problem and shows how the problem is solved. The story is usually told in time order.

Parts of a Fictional Narrative

* A plot with a beginning, middle, and end
* A beginning that introduces the characters, setting, and problem
* Dialogue that shows what is happening or how the characters are feeling
* Strong action words and vivid descriptions
* An ending that shows how the problem is solved

Mystery at Midnight

Beginning Introduces the characters, setting, and problem

Knock! Knock!

I pulled my bed covers up to my chin. What was that noise? I listened closely. Then I heard the strange sounds again. *Knock! Knock!*

"Jason!" I screamed. "Jason, come quick!"

My older brother opened my bedroom door.

Dialogue tells more about what is happening and how the characters are feeling.

"Geez, Mindy," he said. "I was asleep! Why are you yelling?"

"I hear strange noises."

"It's probably just the tree branches scraping your window." He yawned.

"No, it's inside my room." I sat up. "Listen."

Other Transitions
First
Next
After that
During
After a while
Meanwhile
Later
Last

Middle Has rising action to make the story more exciting

Then I heard the noise again, but this time it wasn't a knock. It sounded like a butterfly was flapping its wings against my closet door. Jason tiptoed into my room. I jumped out of bed and stood next to him. "Did you hear that?" I asked.

"Yes," he whispered. "I think it's coming from in there." He pointed to my closet. Then he put his hand on the door knob. He slowly opened the closet door.

Strong action words and vivid descriptions create a clear picture for readers.

"Well, thank goodness!" a little voice said. "I've been trapped in there for hours!" Jason and I peeked into the closet. A small girl stood on one of my hangers. She was only six inches tall, and she had long, curly hair and two golden wings.

"Who are you?" I asked. "And why are you in my closet?"

"I'm the tooth fairy," she said with a smile. "I came to get your tooth, but I was a little early. I decided to hide in your closet until you went to sleep. Then you closed the door, and I got locked inside."

"Oops," I said. "Sorry about that!"

Ending Tells how the story worked out or how the problem is solved

"It's okay," she said. "But now I'm late." She flew across the room and wiggled under my pillow. When she came out, she held my tooth in her hand. "Thanks for this," she said. "Your prize is under your pillow. Now how do I get out of here?"

Jason walked to my bedroom window and opened it. The little fairy flew to it, and then she stopped and winked. "See you next time!" she said. She flew away.

"Wow," Jason said. "That was crazy!" And we both began to laugh.

130 • Grade 3

Fictional Narrative • 131

Minilesson 117

Understanding the Fictional Narrative

Common Core State Standards: W.3.3a, W.3.3b

Objective: Understand characteristics of a fictional narrative.

Guiding Question: How do I write a make-believe story?

Teach/Model

Read the information and student model on pp. 130–131. Add that vivid details help the reader understand the plot and characters; they also add interest to the story. For example, *pulled my bed covers up to my chin* shows that the character was afraid and is more interesting than simply stating, "I was scared."

Practice/Apply

Have pairs of students identify examples of vivid details that make the story interesting. Discuss how the details improve the story.

Minilesson 118

Using Dialogue to Characterize

Common Core State Standard: W.3.3b

Objective: Understand how dialogue reveals characters.

Guiding Question: What can the characters' words show about them?

Teach/Model

Review pp. 130–131. Point out that dialogue is used to help tell the story. Explain that the dialogue reveals the characters' personalities and feelings; it shows who they are. Point out how varied sentence structure in the dialogue shows characters' emotions and helps their words sound natural.

Practice/Apply

Have students point out examples of dialogue that show the characters' personalities and feelings.

Play

Play

A **play** is a story that is acted out in front of an audience. It uses dialogue, or what the characters say to each other, to tell a story.

Parts of a Play

- A list of characters and a description of the setting
- Dialogue between two or more characters
- A beginning, middle, and end to the story
- Descriptions of what characters are doing

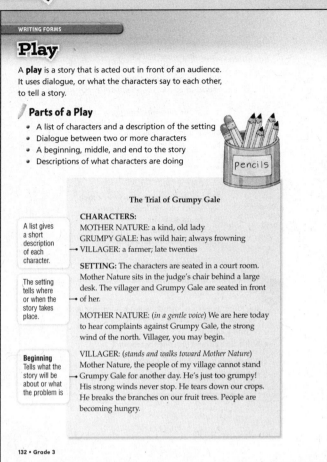

Pencils

The Trial of Grumpy Gale

A list gives a short description of each character.

CHARACTERS:
MOTHER NATURE: a kind, old lady
GRUMPY GALE: has wild hair; always frowning
→ VILLAGER: a farmer; late twenties

The setting tells where or when the story takes place.

SETTING: The characters are seated in a court room. Mother Nature sits in the judge's chair behind a large desk. The villager and Grumpy Gale are seated in front of her.

MOTHER NATURE: (*in a gentle voice*) We are here today to hear complaints against Grumpy Gale, the strong wind of the north. Villager, you may begin.

Beginning
Tells what the story will be about or what the problem is

→ VILLAGER: (*stands and walks toward Mother Nature*) Mother Nature, the people of my village cannot stand Grumpy Gale for another day. He's just too grumpy! His strong winds never stop. He tears down our crops. He breaks the branches on our fruit trees. People are becoming hungry.

132 • Grade 3

Details about what the characters are doing are put inside *parentheses*.

GRUMPY GALE: (*stands and speaks loudly*) I object! The people need to understand that I am very powerful. I must be strong to do my job well.

VILLAGER: But you are too strong! Mother Nature, please! Make Grumpy Gale take a vacation!

GRUMPY GALE: A vacation? Never!

MOTHER NATURE: Now, now, I'm sure I can come up with something to make you both happy. Gale, you used to be a gentle breeze. Do you remember that? You had so much fun making kites fly.

GRUMPY GALE: (*mumbling*) Yes, it was nice then. (*Loudly*) But I also like to be strong and powerful!

Middle
Develops the story and tells more about the problem

→ MOTHER NATURE: I think you can do both. In the fall and winter, you can be a strong and powerful wind. Then, in the spring and summer, you need to rest. You need to become a gentle breeze.

VILLAGER: That's a wonderful idea! The people in the village would be happy to have a gentle breeze.

MOTHER NATURE: Grumpy Gale, do you agree?

GRUMPY GALE: (*in a low, grumpy voice*) I guess so. It might be nice to fly a kite again.

End
Wraps up the story and tells how the problem is solved

→ MOTHER NATURE: Good, it's settled! Now, shake hands and go home. (*The villager and Grumpy Gale shake hands and leave the courtroom.*)

Play • 133

WRITING MODELS AND FORMS

Minilesson 119

Understanding the Play

Common Core State Standard: W.3.4

Objective: Understand the components of a play.

Guiding Question: How is a play different than a narrative?

Teach/Model

Read the definition and student model on pp. 132–133. Explain that the names in all capital letters show the character who is speaking. That name is followed by a colon and the words the character speaks. Point out that stage directions are written in parentheses and that they indicate what the characters do or how they speak; they are not read aloud.

Practice/Apply

Have small groups compare and contrast plays and fictional narratives. Invite students to share their ideas.

Minilesson 120

Organizing a Play

Common Core State Standard: W.3.3b

Objective: Understand how story elements are organized in a play.

Guiding Question: How does a play tell all of the ideas found in a story?

Teach/Model

Review pp. 132–133. Explain that a play includes the same kind of story as a fictional narrative and is organized into a beginning, middle, and end. However, the ideas are not in paragraph form.

Practice/Apply

Have students locate story elements in the play. Discuss how these would be presented in prose.

Poem

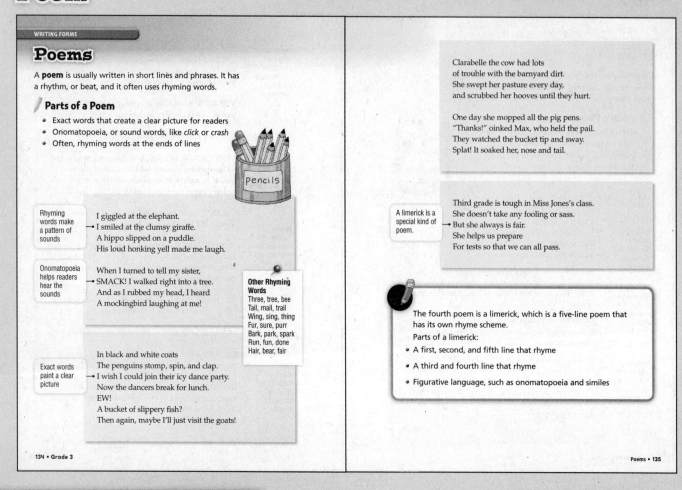

Minilesson 121

Understanding the Poem

Common Core State Standard: W.3.10

Objective: Use the ideas on the pages to understand poems.

Guiding Question: How do I write my ideas as poetry?

Teach/Model

Read the information and sample poems on pp. 134–135. Point out that, when a poem rhymes, the rhyming words create a pattern. Add that the ideas in a poem often continue onto more than one line. Point out that the first two lines of the penguin poem are parts of the same sentence.

Practice/Apply

Have students tell which sample poem does not rhyme. Then have students identify rhyming words in the other poems and explain the patterns they create.

Minilesson 122

Using Onomatopoeia

Common Core State Standard: W.3.10

Objective: Recognize the use of onomatopoeia.

Guiding Question: How are sound words used in poetry?

Teach/Model

Point out the word *SMACK* in the first sample poem on p. 134. Explain that words that imitate sounds are called *onomatopoeia*. These words add interest to writing and help readers hear the action.

Practice/Apply

Have students look for other examples of onomatopoeia on pp. 134–135 (*oinked, splat*). Then have students suggest other examples (ex: *hiss, pop, honk, boom*).

Opinion Essay

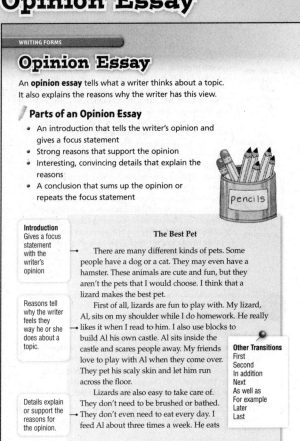

WRITING FORMS

Opinion Essay

An **opinion essay** tells what a writer thinks about a topic. It also explains the reasons why the writer has this view.

Parts of an Opinion Essay

- An introduction that tells the writer's opinion and gives a focus statement
- Strong reasons that support the opinion
- Interesting, convincing details that explain the reasons
- A conclusion that sums up the opinion or repeats the focus statement

Introduction
Gives a focus statement with the writer's opinion

Reasons tell why the writer feels they way he or she does about a topic.

Details explain or support the reasons for the opinion.

The Best Pet

There are many different kinds of pets. Some people have a dog or a cat. They may even have a hamster. These animals are cute and fun, but they aren't the pets that I would choose. I think that a lizard makes the best pet.

First of all, lizards are fun to play with. My lizard, Al, sits on my shoulder while I do homework. He really likes it when I read to him. I also use blocks to build Al his own castle. Al sits inside the castle and scares people away. My friends love to play with Al when they come over. They pet his scaly skin and let him run across the floor.

Lizards are also easy to take care of. They don't need to be brushed or bathed. They don't even need to eat every day. I feed Al about three times a week. He eats

Other Transitions
First
Second
In addition
Next
As well as
For example
Later
Last

fruits, vegetables, and mealworms from the pet store. But the best part is that I don't have to worry about Al if I go away for the weekend. He's happy in his cage as long as it's clean and warm and there's water for him to drink.

Finally, it doesn't cost a lot to own a lizard. Lizards don't need toys or big bags of food. This can save you a lot of money at the pet store! And lizards don't need shots or special medicine. Al is three years old, but he's never had to go to the doctor. In fact, I can go for months without spending one penny on Al.

Dogs, cats, and hamsters make good pets. But the greatest pet is a lizard. If you don't believe me, just ask Al.

Conclusion
Repeats the focus statement in a new way

Note how the author of this piece:

- Wrote a conclusion that re-stated the opinion in a new way. Other ways to end an essay include summing up the reasons for the opinion or giving a final thought.
  Lizards are fun, easy, and inexpensive.
  I have enjoyed owning a lizard more than any other pet.

- Used interesting details to explain the reasons for her opinion.
  My lizard, Al, sits on my shoulder while I do homework.
  I feed Al about three times a week. He eats fruits, vegetables, and mealworms from the pet store.
  Lizards don't need toys or big bags of food.

WRITING MODELS AND FORMS

Minilesson 123

Understanding the Opinion Essay

Common Core State Standards: W.3.1a, W.3.1c

Objective: Understand what is needed in a strong opinion essay.

Guiding Question: How can I tell readers what I think?

Teach/Model

Read and discuss pp. 136–137. Point out that the introduction grabs readers' interest by discussing other pets first. Then the opinion is clearly stated so readers know exactly how the writer feels. Add that the writer's voice helps show his or her feelings.

Practice/Apply

Have students identify the opinion. Then ask them to find reasons that support the opinion and details that help explain the reasons.

Minilesson 124

Including Supporting Reasons

Common Core State Standard: W.3.1c

Objective: Use strong supporting reasons.

Guiding Question: How can I choose which supporting reasons to include?

Teach/Model

Explain that, to explain an opinion, the writer selected strong supporting reasons that might be interesting and meaningful to the audience. The reasons were then organized from most important (lizards are fun) to least (lizards are inexpensive).

Practice/Apply

Have students discuss what reasons might convince an audience of adults that lizards make great pets (ex: they are quiet, they don't have to be walked at night).

Persuasive Essay

Persuasive Essay

A **persuasive essay** tries to convince readers to agree with a writer's opinion. The writer gives reasons to convince readers to take action or think a certain way.

Parts of a Persuasive Essay

- An introduction that tells the writer's opinion and goal
- Reasons that tell why readers should agree with the writer's opinion
- Details, facts, or examples that explain each reason
- A conclusion that sums up the writer's goal or reasons

Introduction
Tells the writer's opinion and goal

The writer gives strong reasons that readers will care about.

School Garden

Our school made a lot of money at the spring carnival. Now the teachers and students have to decide how to spend it. Last night, I came up with a great idea. The money should be used to start a school garden.

First, a school garden will make recess better. Not all kids like playing tag and handball. Usually these kids just talk or read a book. But the garden would give them something fun to do. They could water the plants. They could pick the ripe vegetables. They might even enjoy digging in the soil and pulling the weeds.

Second, a school garden will help students learn. The science teacher, Ms. Peabody, said she would use the school garden to teach about different

Other Transitions
To start with
Then
In addition
Next
As well as
For example
Later
Finally

Details, facts, and examples explain or support the reasons.

The strongest reason usually goes last.

Conclusion
Sums up the writer's goal and reasons

kinds of plants. She also said that the garden would be a good place to do experiments. And that's not all! The health teacher could use the vegetables in the garden to teach students about healthy eating. The math teacher might even be able to use seeds from the garden to make counting and multiplication games. Students would have a great time learning in these ways.

Finally, a school garden could help raise money. The teachers and students could pick flowers and vegetables from the garden each week. Then they could sell them at the farmers' market. The money we make could pay for things like books and markers. It could also be used to buy more seeds and plants.

Building a school garden is the best way to spend the money that we made at the spring carnival. It will make recess better, help students learn, and raise even more money for the school. Everybody wins with a school garden!

Note how the author of this piece:

- Gave reasons that readers will care about.
- Another way the writer could have connected with readers is by answering any questions or concerns they might have.
- Some people think that we don't have the space for a school garden. But that's not true! The open field behind the basketball courts is the perfect place for a garden.
- You might be wondering how long it will take to build the school garden. If everyone works together, we could do it in a week.

WRITING MODELS AND FORMS

Minilesson 125

Understanding the Persuasive Essay

Common Core State Standards: W.3.1a, W.3.1b

Objective: Recognize the qualities of a good persuasive essay.

Guiding Question: How do I convince readers to agree with me?

Teach/Model

Read and discuss pp. 138–139. Point out that the writer included reasons that are important to both teachers and students, since the writer wanted both groups to agree with the opinion.

Practice/Apply

Have students point out which reasons would be important to teachers and which reasons would be important to students.

Minilesson 126

Writing a Strong Goal Statement

Common Core State Standard: W.3.1a

Objective: Recognize characteristics of a strong goal statement.

Guiding Question: What makes a strong goal statement?

Teach/Model

Point out that the last sentence of the first paragraph states the opinion the writer wants readers to agree with. Tell students that words such as *should, need to,* and *best* are often used to convince readers.

Practice/Apply

Have students suggest ways to restate *Having a garden is good* as a strong goal statement (ex: *Planting a garden is the best way to have plenty of fresh vegetables*).

Response to a Play

WRITING FORMS

Response to a Play

A **response to a play** tells about a play that you've read or seen. It tells what the play is like and what you think about it.

Parts of a Response to a Play

- An interesting introduction that mentions the title
- A focus statement that gives an opinion about a character or what happens in the play
- Details and examples from the play that support the opinion
- A conclusion that sums up the response

pencils

Introduction
Includes the title of the play and a focus statement

Details and examples back up the writer's opinion and ideas.

Monkey Tales

Have you ever felt like you don't fit in? Marvin the Monkey sure has! He is one of the characters in <u>Monkey Tales</u>. This funny and silly play shows just how different Marvin is from other monkeys.

To start, Marvin doesn't like bananas. He says that they feel mushy in his mouth. The other monkeys make fun of Marvin. They say he is a snob. This makes Marvin feel bad. But then he comes up with an idea. He makes crispy garlic bread and spaghetti. The other monkeys try his food and love it. They say, "Marvin may be different, but he sure is a good cook!"

Marvin is also scared to swing from trees. He's worried that he'll fall down. He says that swinging makes him sick. The other jungle animals try to teach Marvin how to swing, but it doesn't do any good.

Other Transitions
First
Second
Then
In addition
Next
So
As well as
Later
Finally

He wants to stick with running instead of swinging. Marvin even has a special pair of shoes that help him sprint around the jungle. This is one of the funniest parts in the play.

The last thing that makes Marvin so different is that he doesn't like sitting around all day like the other monkeys do. He wants to be a bus driver instead. He thinks it would be fun to drive around the jungle and meet new animals. Pepper Parrot tells Marvin that monkeys can't drive. But Marvin doesn't care. He says that everyone should have a dream.

<u>Monkey Tales</u> was the best play I have ever read! I loved how silly Marvin was. But the best thing about the play was that it showed that it's okay to be different. Maybe the play should get a new title: <u>The Tale of the Misfit Monkey</u>.

Conclusion
Sums up the response and gives a final thought

Note how the author of this piece:

- Ordered his ideas in a way that makes sense. Good ways to organize a response essay include:
  - Moving from the least important idea to the most important
  - Moving from the most important idea to the least important
  - Giving examples from the selection in time order
- Used connecting words to link the paragraphs.
  To start, Marvin doesn't like bananas.
  Marvin is also scared to swing from trees.
  The last thing that makes Marvin so different is that he doesn't like sitting around all day like the other monkeys do.

WRITING MODELS AND FORMS

Minilesson 127

Understanding the Play Response

Common Core State Standards: W.3.1a, W.3.1b

Objective: Understand the characteristics of a strong response to a play.

Guiding Question: How do I share information about a play?

Teach/Model

Read and discuss pp. 140–141. Point out that this response gets readers interested by beginning with a question that helps readers relate to the story.

Practice/Apply

Have students identify the writer's opinion and locate details and examples that support it.

Minilesson 128

Writing Play Titles

Common Core State Standard: W.3.5

Objective: Underline or italicize play titles.

Guiding Question: What is the correct way to write the title of a play?

Teach/Model

Point out that the writer of the sample essay underlined the title of the play. Explain that book and play titles are printed in italics when they are typed or printed on a computer; they are underlined when the piece of writing is handwritten.

Practice/Apply

Have students identify examples of underlined play titles in the essay and write a few examples of others.

Response to Poetry

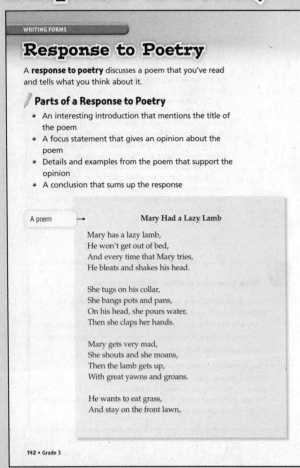

Response to Poetry

A **response to poetry** discusses a poem that you've read and tells what you think about it.

Parts of a Response to Poetry

- An interesting introduction that mentions the title of the poem
- A focus statement that gives an opinion about the poem
- Details and examples from the poem that support the opinion
- A conclusion that sums up the response

A poem →

Mary Had a Lazy Lamb

Mary has a lazy lamb,
He won't get out of bed,
And every time that Mary tries,
He bleats and shakes his head.

She tugs on his collar,
She bangs pots and pans,
On his head, she pours water,
Then she claps her hands.

Mary gets very mad,
She shouts and she moans,
Then the lamb gets up,
With great yawns and groans.

He wants to eat grass,
And stay on the front lawn,

Mary has to go to school,
But there's grass to munch on.

"The walk is too long!"
The lazy lamb cries,
Mary tugs on his leash,
She pulls and she sighs.

She is late for school,
She misses a test,
The lazy lamb naps,
"I need plenty of rest!"

"Make all the children laugh and play,
My friends are very shy!"
The lamb ignores Mary's pleas,
And makes a young boy cry.

The lamb sleeps on a girl's lunch,
And ruins all the food,
So Mary shares her sandwich,
And everything tastes good.

But now Mary is hungry,
Her stomach growls all day,
Soon the school day ends,
But now the sky is gray.

Mary pulls the lamb's leash,
She feels like a great fool,
"That's it!" she cries, "Never again,
Will I bring my lazy lamb to school!"

continued

Minilesson 129

Understanding Rhyme and Meter

Common Core State Standards: W.3.1a, W.3.1b

Objective: Understand poetry.

Guiding Question: How do I tell my ideas about a poem?

Teach/Model

Have students look at the poem on pp. 142–143. Point out the rhyming lines in each stanza. Help students count the beats in each line. Tell them that many poems have rhyme and a certain number of beats per line, called meter.

Practice/Apply

Have students pick a few stanzas from the poem and practice finding rhyming lines and counting out the beats. Discuss how rhyme and meter make the poem sound more rhythmic and make the writing more interesting.

Minilesson 130

Giving an Opinion

Common Core State Standard: W.3.5

Objective: Give an opinion in a response to poetry.

Guiding Question: How do I show how I felt about a poem?

Teach/Model

Have students look at the poem on pp. 142–143. Ask them how they feel about the poem. Do they think it is funny or silly? Do they like it? What do they think of the rhyme scheme? Tell them that they can use what they think about the poem to write an opinion in their response.

Practice/Apply

Have students work in small groups to write an opinion statement about the poem, such as *We really like the poem because the lamb is very funny.*

Response to Poetry

Introduction
Includes the title of the poem and an opinion about it

Mary Had a Lazy Lamb

If you've ever had a bad day, you will love the poem "Mary Had a Lazy Lamb." The poem tells about Mary's very bad day. And it's all because of her lazy lamb.

First, Mary's lamb won't get out of bed in the morning. Mary pulls on his collar. She bangs pots and pans. She pours water on his face. Mary gets very mad. The lamb finally gets up, but he groans a lot. I thought this would make Mary's day better. But her problems are just beginning.

Body
Includes details and examples that back up the writer's opinion

Next, Mary's lamb won't follow her to school. He wants to stay in Mary's front yard and eat grass instead. He says that the walk is too long. Mary has to put a leash on the lamb and drag him to school. This makes Mary so late for school that she misses a test. I felt very bad for Mary!

Then Mary's lazy lamb causes more trouble. Mary says her friends are shy. She wants the lamb to make them laugh and

Other Transitions
To start with
Second
Then
In addition
Next
So
As well as
Later
Last

play. But the lamb does something very different. He makes a boy cry! Then the lamb takes a nap on someone's lunch. The lunch is ruined, so Mary shares her sandwich. This leaves Mary feeling hungry. The poem says that, "her stomach growls all day."

Finally, Mary's lamb won't walk home after school. Mary feels very foolish. She says, "That's it! Never again will I bring my lazy lamb to school."

The writer shares thoughts and feelings about the poem.

I think that "Mary Had a Lazy Lamb" is a very funny poem. I could tell Mary got very mad at her lamb. That lamb was a lot of trouble!

Conclusion
Sums up the response and gives a final thought

I'm sure you will enjoy this poem, too. Mary had a rough day with her lazy lamb. I felt bad for her, but I laughed, too. The poem sure makes me feel that my bad days aren't so bad after all.

Note how the author of this piece:

- Ordered her ideas in a way that makes sense. Good ways to organize a response essay include:
  – Moving from the least important idea to the most important
  – Moving from the most important idea to the least important
  – Giving examples from the selection in time order
- Used a strong transition at the beginning of each paragraph.
  First, Mary's lamb won't get out of bed in the morning.
  Next, Mary's lamb won't follow her to school.
  Finally, Mary's lamb won't walk home after school.

WRITING MODELS AND FORMS

Minilesson 131

Understanding the Response to Poetry

Common Core State Standards: W.3.1a, W.3.1b

Objective: Use the information to understand a response to poetry.

Guiding Question: How do I tell my ideas about a poem?

Teach/Model

Read the definition, poem, and response on pp. 142–145. Point out the writer's opinion in the introduction to the response. Add that a writer can include other opinions and ideas throughout the response.

Practice/Apply

Have students identify the writer's opinions in the response (ex: *I thought this would make Mary's day better; I felt very bad for Mary!*)

Minilesson 132

Using Quotation Marks

Common Core State Standard: W.3.5

Objective: Use quotation marks around titles and quotes.

Guiding Question: How do I show the exact words from a text?

Teach/Model

Point out that the writer used quotation marks around the title of the poem in the introduction of the response. Explain that titles of short works, such as poems, stories, and songs, are written in quotation marks. Add that any exact words from the poem should also be in quotation marks.

Practice/Apply

Have students locate words in the response that have been quoted directly from the poem.

Author Response

Author Response

An **author response** compares two stories or books written by the same author.

Parts of an Author Response Essay

- An introduction to the main characters
- A brief review of the plot for each story
- A review of the similarities and differences in the two stories

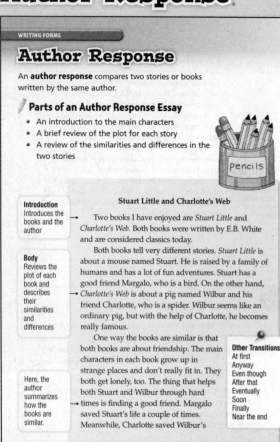

Stuart Little and Charlotte's Web

Introduction
Introduces the books and the author

Two books I have enjoyed are *Stuart Little* and *Charlotte's Web*. Both books were written by E.B. White and are considered classics today.

Body
Reviews the plot of each book and describes their similarities and differences

Both books tell very different stories. *Stuart Little* is about a mouse named Stuart. He is raised by a family of humans and has a lot of fun adventures. Stuart has a good friend Margalo, who is a bird. On the other hand, *Charlotte's Web* is about a pig named Wilbur and his friend Charlotte, who is a spider. Wilbur seems like an ordinary pig, but with the help of Charlotte, he becomes really famous.

Here, the author summarizes how the books are similar.

One way the books are similar is that both books are about friendship. The main characters in each book grow up in strange places and don't really fit in. They both get lonely, too. The thing that helps both Stuart and Wilbur through hard times is finding a good friend. Margalo saved Stuart's life a couple of times. Meanwhile, Charlotte saved Wilbur's

Other Transitions
At first
Anyway
Even though
After that
Eventually
Soon
Finally
Near the end

life many times and taught him that everyone is special, even a pig.

In this paragraph, the author examines how the two books are different.

Stuart Little and *Charlotte's Web* have many things in common. But they also have several things that are quite different. One way they are different is the way each book ends. In *Stuart Little*, the book ends by Stuart going to look for his good friend Margalo. The story doesn't feel finished, and the reader has to imagine what might happen next. On the other hand, *Charlotte's Web* has a great ending. Though Wilbur was sad when Charlotte died, everything worked out in the end. Charlotte had little baby spiders that stayed with Wilbur and became his friends.

Both books are very well-written. E.B. White is a great author. His characters are very lifelike, and there is a lot of emotion in his writing. I got really sad when Charlotte died at the end of *Charlotte's Web*. This is a good sign of a great writer. E.B. White is good at describing feelings.

Conclusion
Summarizes the books and gives an opinion about them

Stuart Little and *Charlotte's Web* are classic novels for kids. All kids should read these novels because they are great stories about friendship. Through these books, E.B. White tells us that everyone is special. Even a pig and a little mouse can teach us how to be nice to each other.

Note how the author of this piece:

- Puts the title of each book in *italics*.
- Tells about what makes the author's books special.
  His characters are very life-like and there is a lot of emotion in his writing.

WRITING MODELS AND FORMS

Minilesson 133

Understanding the Author Response

Common Core State Standards: W.3.2a, W.3.2b

Objective: Recognize the components of an author response.

Guiding Question: How do I compare two books by the same writer?

Teach/Model

Read and discuss pp. 146–147. Explain that a response includes facts about the books and their author as well as the writer's opinion. A response can help readers decide whether or not they would like to read books by this author.

Practice/Apply

Have small groups complete a Venn diagram comparing the two books. They should use only the ideas included in the author response.

Minilesson 134

Showing Similarities and Differences

Common Core State Standard: W.3.2c

Objective: Use words to signal similarities and differences.

Guiding Question: How can I point out ways that two things are alike or different?

Teach/Model

Explain that words such as *both*, *also*, and *likewise* show how two things are similar, or alike. Words such as *on the other hand*, *unlike*, and *however* point out differences.

Practice/Apply

Have students identify words in the student model that signal similarities and differences. Discuss other words that could replace them (ex: replace *On the other hand* with *but*).

Book Review

Book Review

A **book review** tells the reader about a book. This type of essay tells about the characters and plot, and the author gives an opinion about the book.

Parts of a Book Review

- An introduction that describes the name of the book and its author
- A body that details the characters, main conflict, and plot
- A conclusion that reviews the main points and explains the author's opinion

Introduction
Tells the title of the book and who wrote it

Body
Explains the book's main characters and plot

Charlotte's Web

The book *Charlotte's Web* by E.B. White is about a pig named Wilbur and his friend Charlotte, who is a spider. It is a great story about friendship.

Most of the book takes place on a farm. A girl named Fern raises Wilbur and takes care of him. Wilbur is a runt and very small for a pig. One day Wilbur is sold to a farm nearby. Fern goes to visit him as often as she can. After some time, Fern can't see Wilbur much, and he starts to get lonely.

One day, while in the barn, Wilbur meets a spider named Charlotte. Charlotte is very smart and full of good advice. Soon Wilbur and Charlotte become very good friends. Wilbur meets a lot of other farm animals, too, including a funny rat named Templeton. Templeton seems pretty selfish, but he has a good heart.

Other Transitions
After some time
One day
Soon
One night
By this time
Before

The conflict is the main problem that needs to be solved by the characters.

This paragraph describes how the characters solved the problem.

This paragraph describes how the story ended.

Conclusion
Reviews the main points of the book and explains why the author liked or disliked the book

One night one of the old sheep tells Wilbur the farmer plans to eat him for Christmas dinner. Wilbur and his friends get very worried. Charlotte then gets an idea to write words in her web about Wilbur. She thinks this idea might save Wilbur.

Templeton helps by getting pieces of newspaper with words on them and gives them to Charlotte. These words are adjectives that describe Wilbur. Charlotte spells out things like "some pig" and "terrific." The farmer notices the words and decides not to eat Wilbur. Instead he brings Wilbur to the county fair. At the fair, Wilbur wins a prize and becomes famous.

By this time Charlotte is really old for a spider. She dies while at the fair with Wilbur. Wilbur is very sad about losing his best friend. Before she died, though, Charlotte left behind a sac of eggs. Wilbur brings the egg sac back to the farm with him. Soon the eggs hatch. Most of the baby spiders leave the farm but three stay behind. They soon become Wilbur's new friends at the farm.

Charlotte's Web is a wonderful book. It is a great story about friendship. I liked a lot of the characters in the book, especially the rat Templeton. My favorite part of the book was all the talking animals. It was very sad when Charlotte died, and I felt bad for Wilbur. But everything worked out in the end, and Wilbur got new friends. E.B. White is a really good writer. This is a great book, and I would tell other people to read it.

Minilesson 135

Understanding the Book Review

Common Core State Standard: W.3.4

Objective: Use the information to understand a book review.

Guiding Question: How do I tell about a book I have read?

Teach/Model

Read the definition, bulleted list, and student model on pp. 148–149. Add that the events included in the review are described in the same order that they occurred in the book. The student writer used transitions to show the order of the events.

Practice/Apply

Have students read the list of Other Transitions and locate these in the review.

Minilesson 136

Summarizing Important Events

Common Core State Standard: W.3.4

Objective: Summarize key details from a book.

Guiding Question: What ideas do I include in a book review?

Teach/Model

Review the sample book review on pp. 148–149. Explain that a book review does not tell all of the events that occurred in the story; it retells, in the writer's own words, the most important things that happened as the characters solved the problem.

Practice/Apply

Have students select and summarize key events from other familiar stories—fairy tales, stories read in class, etc. Remind students to focus on only three or four of the most important events.

Persuasive Speech

WRITING FORMS

Persuasive Speech

A **persuasive speech** tries to convince an audience about something. The author uses facts to argue his or her opinion about a subject.

Parts of a Persuasive Speech
- An introduction that describes the main arguments
- Supporting arguments backed up with details or facts
- A conclusion that restates the main argument and supporting ideas

Introduction
Tells the subject and the author's main arguments

Body
Gives details and facts that support the author's arguments

Each body paragraph gives details about one topic.

Why We Should Get a Cat

I think that getting a cat is a great idea. Cats are very easy to take care of. They are also fun to have around the house. Owning a cat would teach me how to be more responsible. There are so many reasons why we should get a cat.

First, cats are not hard to take care of. Unlike some animals, cats only need food twice a day. Dogs eat lots of dog food and human food. They will eat anything they can get their paws on! On the other hand, cats only eat about a half a cup of cat food a day. That will save money and time. Cats also save time because they take care of themselves. They lick themselves to stay clean, so you will not have to give them a bath. They also don't need to be taken for a walk. Cats can do so much on their own!

Second, cats are lots of fun. They like to play with toys. You don't even need to

Other Transitions
Although
Sometimes
After that
Once in a while
Even though
Meanwhile
Lastly
In closing

spend much money to keep them busy. A simple piece of yarn will make a cat run, leap, and roll. Although they have a lot of energy, they also like to relax. A cat is like a cuddly blanket. When it is chilly outside, a cat will keep you warm by sitting on your lap.

Finally, a good reason to get a cat is that I could learn about responsibility. You might be wondering who will take care of the cat. Even though cats do not take much time, parents are still very busy and might not have time for a pet. However, you don't have to worry. I would be the person who takes care of the cat. I would feed the cat twice a day. I would also change the kitty litter. Having a cat would teach me how to take care of things.

There are so many reasons why we should get a cat. What other pet is so easy and fun? I know you agree that a cat will be a perfect pet for our family. Let's go pick one out today!

Conclusion
Reviews the writer's opinions and makes a final statement

Note how the author of this piece:

- Answers a question that her audience might have.
  You might be wondering who will take care of the cat…
  I would be the person who takes care of the cat.

- Ends her speech with an encouraging statement.
  Other ways she could have ended her speech are to give a fact or a quote.
  Scientists say that people with cats often live longer because cats are so relaxing.
  As Charles Dickens said, "What greater gift than the love of a cat?"

WRITING MODELS AND FORMS

Minilesson 137

Understanding the Persuasive Speech

Common Core State Standards: W.3.1a, W.3.1b

Objective: Use the pages to understand a persuasive speech.
Guiding Question: How do I convince an audience?

Teach/Model
Read and discuss pp. 150–151. Point out that the main arguments are introduced at the very beginning. Each of the following paragraphs explains one of the arguments and includes supporting facts and details.

Practice/Apply
Have students identify each argument stated in the introduction and then locate the paragraph that supports it. Have students identify the facts and details that offer the strongest argument.

Minilesson 138

Selecting Convincing Details

Common Core State Standard: W.3.1b

Objective: Choose details that will persuade readers.
Guiding Question: What should I say to convince the audience to agree with me?

Teach/Model
Point out that the writer only included details that would convince the audience to agree that getting a cat is a good idea. The writer left out details that might cause people to disagree, such as that cats sometimes scratch people and vet bills can be expensive.

Practice/Apply
Have students find details in the speech that explain why getting a cat is a good idea; then have them suggest details that support the opposite opinion.

Labels and Captions

Labels and Captions

A **label** tells what a picture is or shows the parts of something. A **caption** adds information to a picture or explains an idea. A label uses one or a few words. A caption includes one or more complete sentences.

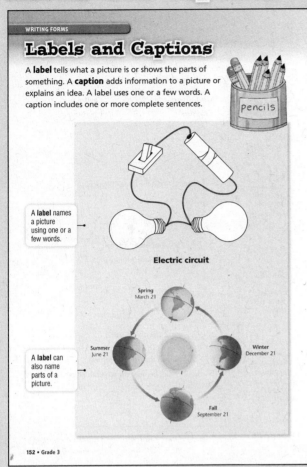

A **label** names a picture using one or a few words.

Electric circuit

A **label** can also name parts of a picture.

Spring
March 21

Summer
June 21

Winter
December 21

Fall
September 21

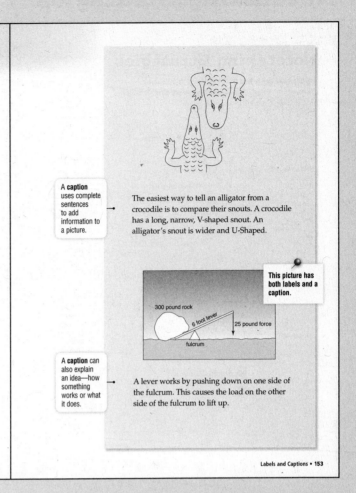

A **caption** uses complete sentences to add information to a picture.

The easiest way to tell an alligator from a crocodile is to compare their snouts. A crocodile has a long, narrow, V-shaped snout. An alligator's snout is wider and U-Shaped.

This picture has both labels and a caption.

300 pound rock

6 foot lever

25 pound force

fulcrum

A **caption** can also explain an idea—how something works or what it does.

A lever works by pushing down on one side of the fulcrum. This causes the load on the other side of the fulcrum to lift up.

Minilesson 139

Understanding Labels and Captions

Common Core State Standards: W.3.2a, W.3.2b

Objective: Understand the use of labels and captions.

Guiding Question: How can I use information about illustrations to help explain a topic?

Teach/Model

Read and discuss pp. 152–153. Add that illustrations help show ideas and information to readers. Labels and captions explain what is shown in the illustration; they also can add information about the subject.

Practice/Apply

Have students compare and contrast the types of information given in labels and captions. Have them discuss situations in which each would be useful.

Minilesson 140

Using Illustrations

Common Core State Standard: W.3.2a

Objective: Recognize that illustrations can aid in comprehension.

Guiding Question: How can I help readers better understand my ideas?

Teach/Model

Review the illustrations on pp. 152–153. Explain that these are the kinds of illustrations a writer might include in order to help readers understand a subject. Add that being able to see what a writer describes often helps the ideas make sense.

Practice/Apply

Have students discuss ways the illustrations on pp. 152–153 could help readers understand information.

Notetaking Strategies

Notetaking Strategies

Notetaking helps you to remember important information. You can take notes while reading, listening, or watching a demonstration or video.

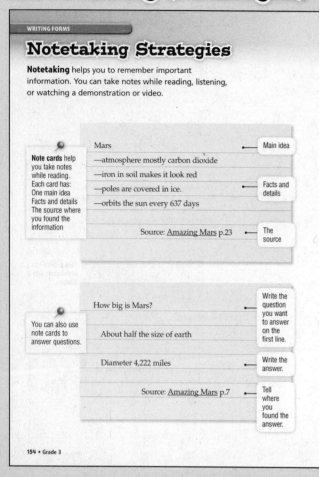

Note cards help you take notes while reading. Each card has: One main idea Facts and details The source where you found the information

Mars
—atmosphere mostly carbon dioxide
—iron in soil makes it look red
—poles are covered in ice.
—orbits the sun every 637 days

Source: _Amazing Mars_ p.23

Main idea

Facts and details

The source

You can also use note cards to answer questions.

How big is Mars?

About half the size of earth

Diameter 4,222 miles

Source: _Amazing Mars_ p.7

Write the question you want to answer on the first line.

Write the answer.

Tell where you found the answer.

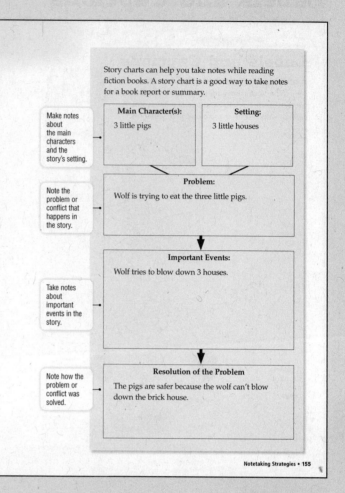

Story charts can help you take notes while reading fiction books. A story chart is a good way to take notes for a book report or summary.

Make notes about the main characters and the story's setting.

Main Character(s):	Setting:
3 little pigs	3 little houses

Note the problem or conflict that happens in the story.

Problem:
Wolf is trying to eat the three little pigs.

Take notes about important events in the story.

Important Events:
Wolf tries to blow down 3 houses.

Note how the problem or conflict was solved.

Resolution of the Problem
The pigs are safer because the wolf can't blow down the brick house.

WRITING MODELS AND FORMS

Minilesson 141

Understanding Notetaking Strategies

Common Core State Standard: W.3.8

Objective: Use the pages to understand how to take notes.

Guiding Question: What can I do to organize information as I read or hear it?

Teach/Model

Read the information and student samples on pp. 154–155. Point out that the strategies on p. 154 are used to record nonfiction information and that the chart on p. 155 is for information from a fiction story.

Practice/Apply

Have students discuss the differences between the note-card strategies and how they might use note cards.

Minilesson 142

Including Information in Notes

Common Core State Standard: W.3.8

Objective: Understand what information to include when taking notes.

Guiding Question: What should I write when taking notes?

Teach/Model

Review the sample note cards on pp. 154–155. Point out that the writer did not include all the information or write in complete sentences. Instead, the notes have only the most interesting or important facts and are made up of only the key words.

Practice/Apply

Have students practice taking notes in phrases instead of in sentences.

Journal

Journal

A **journal** is a notebook in which you can write about anything you want. You can tell a true story about your life. You can tell your thoughts and feelings. Often, you are the only one to read your journal.

Parts of a Journal Entry

- The date at the top of the page
- A beginning that tells what the entry is about
- Interesting, important details that show your thoughts and feelings
- Informal words and phrases that sound like you
- The pronouns *I*, *me*, and *we*

pencils

Beginning
Perhaps tells about an important event or main idea

March 24

Today I got the best surprise ever! Mom took me to an amusement park. It was just the two of us. We had a great day!

As soon as we got there, we met my favorite fairy tale hero. She was really pretty and talked with a funny accent. She told us some of her adventures. It was awesome!

Details show why the event was important and how you felt.

When that was over, we went on the bumper cars. I was super excited because I got to steer. Mom pushed the pedals. I was not tall enough to reach. Mom called me "Peanut"! I'm really good at steering, but I made Mom think I wasn't so that I could drive into the other cars. It was a lot of fun!

Other Journal Uses
Brainstorming
Sketching
Diary Entries
Notetaking
Rough drafts
Definitions
Memories
Learning Log

Pronouns *I*, *me*, and *we* show that it is about you or someone else.

After that we went on the spinning tea cups. We went pretty fast. It was fun! Afterward, I was so dizzy I could hardly walk.

I was not too dizzy for a snack, though! We got chocolate space ice cream. That was really cool. It's not like normal ice cream. It looks like rocks or pebbles, but it tastes really good.

I wanted to go on the roller coasters, but I'm still too short for those. Mom says maybe next year I'll be tall enough. The roller coasters look really fun! Mom doesn't like roller coasters because she is afraid of heights. But I can't wait until I'm tall enough!

It was great to spend time with Mom and to try all these fun rides. Maybe next time we'll bring Dad and Joey. I'd like to take my friend Samantha, too.

It was a really great day! I hope we go back many times this summer.

Ending
Wraps up the journal entry

Note how the author of this piece:

- Wrote about something that happened to her.

  She also could have used her journal to write about something she learned in school.

  Today we studied Helen Keller in history class. I think she was a really interesting person.

- Included plenty of details about what happened.

  She was really pretty and talked with a funny accent.
  It looks like rocks or pebbles, but it tastes really good.

Minilesson 143

Understanding the Journal Entry

Common Core State Standard: W.3.3b

Objective: Understand how to use the information about a journal entry that is presented in the lesson.

Guiding Question: What belongs in a journal entry?

Teach/Model

Read the definition, bulleted points, and model on pp. 156–157. Point out that a journal is a kind of notebook and that a journal entry represents one or two pages from the book. Explain that stories usually have a title but that journal entries have a date in place of a title.

Practice/Apply

Have students locate the parts of a journal entry mentioned in the bulleted list.

Minilesson 144

Using Details

Common Core State Standard: W.3.3b

Objective: Select details to include in a journal entry.

Guiding Question: What details should I write in my journal?

Teach/Model

Explain that the purpose of a journal entry is to write about events and experiences so the writer can remember them at a later time. Tell students that, for a journal entry, they will want to put down exactly what happened, what they saw, and how they felt about it.

Practice/Apply

Have students write one more detail to show how the writer may have felt that day.

Common Core Writing • 115

Index